Coaching Days in the Midlands

by Brian Haughton

The inns, coaches, horses, highwaymen
and the terrible roads. How the Midlands
developed its road network, and the
glory days of the stage coach.

****

Quercus
John Roberts
8 Hillside Close, Bartley Green
Birmingham B32 4LT

****

Coaching Days in the Midlands

by Brian Haughton

ISBN 1 898136 13 0

First Published 1997

Preface

QuercuS specialises in publishing books about the western Midlands, or the area between the rivers Trent, Severn and Avon that geographers call the "Midland Triangle". Titles include *Midland Woods & Forests, Midland Rivers, Midland Ghosts & Hauntings, Midland Castles, Historic Houses & Gardens, Heart in my Boots* and albums of pen and ink sketches of buildings in Hales Owen, Bromsgrove and Birmingham. Coming soon are *Midland Murders & Mysteries* and *Midland Spirits & Spectres*.

It was seeing some earlier QuercuS books that prompted Brian Haughton to approach me about a book based on his research into coaching in this area. It seemed likely to fit well with the rest of my plans, and I am very happy to present Brian's fascinating work.

The Author

BRIAN HAUGHTON was born in Birmingham in 1964. Whilst working for the civil service he took a holiday in Crete, where the Bronze Age palace of Knossos sparked his interest in archaeology. This led him to Nottingham University, from where he emerged in 1994 with a degree in archaeology. He has since worked on excavations in England and Greece. Brian is now studying for a Masters Degree in Greek archaeology at Birmingham University. This book sprang from his long term interest in local history and from a glimpse of the stage coach in Birmingham Museum and Art Gallery.

Thank you to ...

Special thanks to Elizabeth Elwell, to Emma Jones of the Warwickshire Sites and Monuments Record Office, to Staffordshire County Museum at Shugborough House, to staff at Ludlow Library, to Irene Cardell for information on Southam, and to Irene de Boo at Birmingham Museum and Art Gallery.

Contents

Introduction

When we travel our roads and motorways these days we rarely think how the people of this country travelled a century or two ago. Yet it is surprising how recollecting the past can enrich the present, especially in relation to travel.

Until quite recently animal haulage, especially by horses and horse drawn vehicles, had been the dominant method of transport in this country since prehistoric times. This book is about one particular form of horse drawn vehicle - the stagecoach. Related forms such as private coaches, omnibuses and carriers' wagons are mentioned only in passing.

The stagecoach is perhaps the most mysterious and romantic of all forms of public conveyance. As Washington Irving put it - *"The stagecoach carries animation always with it, and puts the world in motion as it whirls along"*. The whole experience is about being in touch with the passing scenery as a result of the combined exertions of man and beast, of blood pumping energy and daring skill. It was as far from the railway that superseded it as the hot air balloon is from the supersonic jet.

Yet its glory days were numbered and its reign short. The stagecoach lasted probably fifty or sixty years as the main form of public transport in this country, and its heyday covered no more than fifteen or twenty (c 1820-1838). It is from these few years that the picture of the stagecoach in the popular imagination derives - from Christmas cards, coaching prints, the works of Dickens and to a lesser extent, Thomas De Quincey and George Eliot.

Documentary evidence of the coaching age is rare, and so are examples of coaches, toll houses, original milestones and other hardware. The only public stagecoach in the Midlands is in the Birmingham Museum and Art Gallery, and that is a late and untypical vehicle which was operated by a Liverpool proprietor between Chester and Shrewsbury. The collections of coaches at Charlecote, near Stratford upon Avon and Shugborough, near Stafford are all of private vehicles and only one, at Shugborough is of the stagecoach type. Considering that there were well over three thousand on the road in the 1830s, this is surprising, but the Victorians were unsentimental about the past and full of confidence in an improving future, something we have lost.

There are no surviving coaching inns in Birmingham and many elsewhere have been rebuilt and survive only in name. The number of books written about coaching is also small, especially compared with the vast number on other types of transport, such as railways and canals.

Perhaps this very elusiveness of material helps to retain the mystique of the stagecoach, which is enhanced by association with an age completely lost to us.

Coach fares and other amounts of money are often mentioned, and are shown in pounds, shillings and pence. We decimalised our currency in 1972 and increasing numbers of people have never experienced this strange system, so here is a quick guide. 12 pennies made 1 shilling, 20 shillings made 1 pound. A shilling was the same as our decimal 5 pence, and 2.4d (old pennies) made 1p. You may find it easiest to think in shillings. Even if you were familiar with £sd, there are problems in estimating equivalent purchasing values because of the staggering loss of value of our currency, especially since the 1950s. A coach fare of £1.10 shillings (now £1.50p - ie 10 x 5p) from Birmingham to London might seem cheap, but Charles Dickens mentioned this as the weekly wage of Scrooge's clerk, Bob Crachit. He was very poor but somehow just kept a large family at starvation level. The modern equivalent in standard of living terms might be someone living on, say, £45 per week. A comparison with modern rail fares (excluding bargains) is revealing. A confusing item is the guinea which sometimes appears as the price paid for a coach or a horse. This was literally £1.1 shilling, a truly British eccentricity. The guinea was actually a gold coin, and the original intention was that the purchaser would hand over a bag of the things for his horse or coach. In practice, by the coaching era the price was as often paid in ordinary currency or by cheque.

Measurements of length are Imperial; routes distances and the dimensions of coaches and so on are in miles, yards, feet and inches. Even youngsters taught in the metric system are familiar with the old, batty, one so we have not offered conversions.

Illustrations for this book presented some problems. Full scale public coaching services had vanished before the invention of photography, but I have used photos by myself and John Roberts, the publisher, of remaining toll houses, milestones and inns, The two photos of surviving stagecoaches came from museums, and we have simple road maps in the early chapters. But these seemed very static pictures for a book whose essence is travel and movement. We were lucky. The all-action local cover picture is a sketch from a painting in Birmingham Museum and Art Gallery which is not currently on display, but was discovered from a postcard. The other sketches are engravings by Hugh Thomson (1860 - 1920) which illustrated a monthly feature called *Coaching Ways and Coaching Days*. Installments appeared in the *The English Illustrated Magazine* during 1888, which came to us as a bound volume through a friend of a friend. These pictures made Thomson's name and his work was in frequent demand for books by authors living and dead, such as Jane Austen, Fanny Burney, Mrs Gaskell, Charles Reade, and J M Barrie.

Photo: Birmingham Museum & Art Gallery

The only stage coach in the Midlands stands in the Birmingham Museum and Art Gallery. It has an ash frame with mahogany panels and could seat 19 passengers. A Liverpool proprietor put on this service in 1860, apparently in competition with the railway which had opened in 1848.

The Transport Revolution

The period from around 1650 to the mid 1830s brought a revolution in British transport, first in roads and later canals. In this revolution the Midland counties played a vital role. Outside London, this is probably the most important area in Britain in terms of transport, since almost any journey north to south or east to west must pass through it.

The state of the roads at the beginning of this period was appalling. An Act of Parliament in 1555 holding each parish responsible for the roads passing through it had made no difference. But with the economy and trade expanding, some system for maintenance and improvement was desperately needed. The solution eventually reached was by way of travellers paying a toll, and this was the begining of the turnpike system.

The first Turnpike Act was passed in 1662 and involved the Great North Road through Hertfordshire and Cambridgeshire. The first Act to affect the Midlands was passed in 1707 and concerned the road from Old Stratford in Northamptonshire to Dunchurch, just south of Rugby. The Acts empowered Turnpike Trusts, which are best seen as local private companies seeking a profit, to build toll gates and houses. The cash collected for roadworks was then applied to the highways with varying degrees of willingness and efficiency.

Despite hoped for improvements, the condition of roads in the early 18th century was little better than it had been a hundred years before. The turnpike system itself was unpopular and seen more as a necessary evil than a potential benefit. However, improvements did come, if slowly, and with the work of the pioneering road builders and engineers Metcalf, Macadam and Telford (the latter responsible for the Holyhead Road) a much improved and fairly efficient network was achieved by the early 1820s.

Official passenger transport in England can be traced back to 1550 when slow stage wagons carried goods and passengers. But as the importance of commerce increased, effective links between towns became a major concern. This was the driving force behind the stagecoach system. The name was derived from the practice of dividing routes into stages, at the end of which horses would be changed and passengers allowed time for meals.

The earliest known "coach" in England was that built in 1555 for the Earl of Rutland by Walter Rippon, whose firm rose to prominence as coachbuilders in the 19th century. The first record of an actual stagecoach is about a century later in 1637, travelling between London and St Albans. The long distance coach which ran between London and Chester by 1659 is particularly relevant in the context of this book. Its route ran through Lichfield and Stone and it is the earliest evidence we have for a stagecoach in the Midlands. Sir William Dugdale in this diary for 1679 mentions what might be the first service into Birmingham: *"I came out of London by the stagecoach of Bermincham to Banbury."*

Much of the coaching business was initiated in the Midlands, as provincial towns were more anxious to link themselves with the trade magnet of London than London was to them. Birmingham, at the centre of the Midlands, swelled in importance after the Industrial Revolution, both as a manufacturing town and as the focus of a road network. The first of many stagecoaches between Birmingham and the capital was put on by Nicholas Rothwell of Warwick, in 1731.

In these early days of coaching though, roads were still inadequate and the unsprung and badly designed vehicles were slow and uncomfortable. Consequently coach travel did not become at all popular until the latter part of the 18th century.

The cumbersome vehicles were easy prey for that most picturesque of criminals, the highwayman. The heyday of this "prince of thieves" lasted roughly the hundred years between 1650 and 1750, though he had not entirely disappeared by the early 19th century. On the whole, far from being the daring champion of the poor popularised in books and films, he was often no more than a cowardly thief and occasionally a cold blooded killer. Yet somehow he still has a hold on our imagination and the myth surrounding him has become almost impossible to dispel.

He was at last put out of business by better road maintenance, permitting faster travel, and the appearance of the Royal Mail coaches with their armed guards.

The first Royal Mail coach appeared on the London to Bristol route in August 1784, the brainchild of John Palmer, a theatre owner from Bath. Previously letters had been carried on horseback by the largely unreliable postboys, who were slow and often robbed. Splendid in black and maroon, with the Royal cipher picked out in gold on the foreboot, the Mails set new standards in coach design, punctuality and reliability. They averaged speeds of 8 to 10 miles per hour, were exempted from tolls and often travelled overnight. All this was not lost on the stagecoach proprietors who had to improve their services in order to compete, and most particularly in speed and efficiency. By the early 1800s stage and mail coaches had become a fashionable if rather expensive way to travel.

The resultant increase in speed and traffic on the roads, combined with natural hazards such as snow and flood, led to accidents. Coachmen drunk at the reins and coaches racing each other were also responsible for their share. We have learned little since.

By the early 1820s the heyday of coaching was underway, the so called golden age. The coaching business had become a major industry and source of employment. By the mid 1830s there were about 3000 stagecoaches, and 261 patent mail coaches (that is - operating under Royal patent, or licence) in regular use in England and Wales. A remarkable organisation of inns and posting houses every 10 or 12 miles along the main routes allowed for changes of horses and refreshments, establishments usually fully or partly owned by coach operators.

Probably the most famous inn of all was the Swan With Two Necks in Lad Lane, London, owned by William Chaplin; without doubt England's most important coaching inn. Edward Sherman was another London proprietor. His Shrewsbury *Wonder* stagecoach became a legend in its own time, mainly due to incredible feats of speed supposed to have been performed on the Holyhead Road. Important provincial towns like Birmingham also had their proprietors, men like William Waddell who in the 1830s owned the town's two most important coaching inns, *The Swan* and *The Hen & Chickens*.

It was unfortunate that the coaching industry reached its zenith just as a more significant revolution in transport was beginning. As early as 1825 there was a railway linking Stockton and Darlington, though it was on too small a scale to affect the coaching business. By the late 1830s though, the transport field was changing rapidly. Experiments with steam railways over longer distances were bringing more and more success. Rail travel was cheaper and often more comfortable than coach travel, and in a short while its journey times made a mockery of those proudly advertised by the coach proprietors.

In 1838 Parliament authorised the carrying of the Mails by rail, and in April of the same year the London & Birmingham Railway opened. It was the beginning of the end for stage and mail coaches. The process by which railway replaced coach transport was relatively slow in some areas, but in places such as Lichfield it happened almost overnight. The effect on the coaching industry was devastating and a whole way of life vanished within a few years. A revival of coaches as pleasure vehicles for the well to do began in the 1860s and carried on intermittently into this century, but as a viable form of public transport the coach had become obsolete.

"The Post Roads of England 1675"
from Ogilvy's "Brittania".

Roads before the Turnpikes

Road management in the Middle Ages was a responsibility of the Manor, which was the main unit for landholding and local administration. However, here and there were instances of particular people charged with the maintenance of certain roads. A surviving example is Clopton Bridge spanning the River Avon at Stratford, which was provided by Sir Hugh Clopton in the late 15th century. Repairs might be done by roadside chaplaincies out of money given as religious offerings. There were even a few cases of tolls collected over short periods by authority of Royal Letters Patent.

As manorial influence declined and as money dedicated for pious uses became diverted to secular purposes, including the financing of wars, there grew up a Common Law obligation on the parishes and townships to maintain their own highways.

The condition of England's roads at this time was quite appalling. Travellers usually needed local guides to get about, and the only lighting at night was by flaming torches for the immediate path, and by beacon fires lit to give general direction. Originally a "road" had meant a right of passage rather than the actual track, and nowhere was this better illustrated than in the open farming areas. One year the approach to the village might be straight-forward across the fallow, but next year the fallow might have been ploughed in long strips separated by balks, or furrow leys, and the traveller might have to make a wide detour.

A witness at the Court of Star Chamber in the reign of James I (1603-1625) testified;

> "Sometymes when the common feilds of Ladbrooke [in Warwickshire] lay open, the passengers did...passe and goe over the said comon feilds...upon one furrow ley and sometymes upon another...but they did notwithstanding usually keep neare one place."

More important routes were usually better provided for. After dissolution of the monastery of Evesham in 1540, the town continued to grow as an important market centre. It was on the main route from London to Worcester and the Welsh Marches, and the wealthy merchants of the town wanted people coming to the markets and fairs to be able to get there.

Dissolution of the monasteries by Henry VIII left their duties unattended and the loss of their guest houses and hospitals (ie. hostels) was a blow to the travelling community. When the buildings and vast landholdings of the religious orders were sold, the new owners did not necessarily follow the example of their predecessors in maintaining the roads.

Such a state of affairs led to the Statute of Philip and Mary,

> "for amending of Highways being both very noissome
> and tedious to travel in and dangerous to all Passengers
> and Carriages".

Passed as a temporary measure, it was re-enacted eight years later by Queen Elizabeth. Under this and its amending Acts, the statute labour system was regulated - a system which remained the basis of highway administration for nearly three centuries.

The Act made each parish responsible for roads passing through it, with each parishioner who kept teams and carts ordered to send them out, and those able bodied who did not to come in person. This labour was to be for not less than eight hours on four (later six) days per year. Women were not at first specifically excluded, but later modifying Acts made it clear that in those rare cases where women were house or freeholders, some exemptions would apply. Some unfortunate was also to be appointed the unpaid surveyor of highways for the parish, and was to levy rates of up to 6d in the pound to buy materials. Parishes that did not meet their obligations were fined at the Quarter Sessions courts.

Under such laws the people of Boscote, near Southam (just south of Leamington) were fined in 1643 for failure to repair the Old Forge Bridge. In 1664 Long Itchington a few miles to the north was in trouble for

> "not repairing the King's Highway lying in the parish and
> leading from the market town of the City of Coventry to
> the market town of Southam."

In parishes with light soils and few roads running through them the system worked tolerably well, and all roads received a share of attention. But in areas of heavy clay soils, like much of the Midlands, and where frequently used routes traversed their parish there was obvious unfairness; the system was unpopular and usually inefficient.

The days of statutory labour were necessarily worked in summer and inevitably interrupted more important work. Labourers either had to go without six day's earnings or hire replacements which they could not afford. Richer farmers and landowners who had to spare horses and carts from their own concerns felt they were being unfairly treated compared with their neighbours. In many parishes by the 18th century, money had been substituted for direct labour.

The main problem lay in the fact that the parishes with main roads running through them were repairing routes used mainly by travellers from outside, whose statutory roads duties would have to be performed elsewhere. Main roads skirting a parish might be used hardly at all by the people who had to maintain them. Parishioners complained and the roads hardly improved.

In Leamington at this time the Old London Road (now High Street) was in parts so dangerous that no wheeled vehicle could use it. In 1575 Queen Elizabeth was journeying from Long Itchington (east of Leamington) but had to travel round via Chesterton and Oakley Wood to reach Warwick, where Robert Dudley, Earl of Leicester was awaiting her.

Roads were best in well drained, stony areas and at their worst in low lying places on clay or marl soils. Plot's account of the Staffordshire roads in 1686 shows why these roads were some of the best in England, but notes that in the south of the county traffic was increasing and roads were degenerating. Most roads had been built, if they had built at all and were not just natural tracks, for pack and riding horses. Their widths, gradients and surface were not suitable for the increasing numbers of wheeled vehicles.

The second half of the 17th century brought a flood of eye witness accounts of road conditions in diaries of travel by Pepys, Evelyn, Thoresby, Celia Fiennes and Sir William Dugdale. All testified to the lamentable condition of most roads. In 1697 Celia Fiennes set out from Warwick to cover the 14 miles to Daventry, "all along part of the Vale of the Red Horse which was very heavy way and could not reach thither". As they reached Shuckborough, only 11 miles from Warwick, night fell and Sir Charles Shuckborough took pity on the exhausted travellers and their horses, "weary with the heavy way."

The ground over much of the Midlands is heavy clay, so many of the roads might have been fair in dry summer months but became quagmires after heavy rainfall. This meant that they could be impassable to wheeled traffic for five or six months of the year. In *A Tour through England and Wales,* written in the 1720s, Daniel Defoe notes the soils of the Midlands as being of "deep stiff clay" and that the:

> "deep clays reach through all the towns of Brickhill, Fenny and Stony Stratford, Towcester, Hill Morton or Dunchurch, Coventry, Coleshill and even to Birmingham, for very nearly 80 miles."

Road repair at the time was primitive. It usually consisted of raking the surface (i.e. the soil), then dumping on it a layer of gravel or stones of mixed shapes, sizes and nature. As the wet weather set in the stones began to sink, the wet soil came up from between them and spread over the surface. Before long wheels began to sink too, and the ruts grew deeper and deeper. Occasionally the roadway would be subjected to a contraption known as the "road plough" before raking, and sometimes stone or brushwood would be laid in the ruts.

There was an obvious need for a complete change of system if trade, commerce and industry were to flourish. What the country needed was a workable system of improving and maintaining existing roads and building reliable new ones. A way of financing this system had also to be found that at least attempted to be fair to all concerned. These needs lead at the end of the 17th century to the Turnpike System.

Toll house on Clopton Bridge, Stratford upon Avon

The Turnpike System

The name "turnpike" derived from the barrier first used to block the road in the very early years of the system. It took the form of a tapered, counterbalanced bar pivoted on a upright post so as to swing horizontally across the road. Possibly, but not certainly, early versions of this barrier were fitted with spikes, or pikes, like those used as defence against cavalry. When the toll was paid the bar was turned, hence "turnpike".

In simple terms a turnpike road meant that a local trust was empowered by Act of Parliament to charge tolls on travellers by erecting toll gates, usually at each end. At cross roads and junctions, side bars were set up on the gates to catch traffic coming onto the turnpike from side roads. Income from the tolls was to be used for repair and maintenance of the road, or sometimes to build a new one.

It was on the Great North Road (from London to York), under an Act of 1663, in the counties of Hertfordshire, Cambridgeshire and Huntingdonshire, that the first three toll gates were erected. Amidst furious opposition from local people, gates were put up at Wadesmill, Caxton and Stilton. Public outcry was such that the gate of Stilton was never put to use and that at Caxton was easily avoided. Wadesmill then, was the site of Britain's first effective toll gate.

Despite this initial activity it was to be over thirty years before the precedent set by this first Turnpike Act was followed, with parts of the London to Harwich road in Essex turnpiked in 1695-1696. Other Turnpike Acts followed and in the Parliamentary session 1706-1707 among the eight Acts for the turnpiking of roads were two which departed from the pattern set by the first few. The earlier Acts had established as turnpike authorities either selected Justices or the County Justices. But these two Acts set up bodies of local gentlemen who were not necessarily justices as trustees or commissioners.

The aim of those setting up the trust was firstly as an investment to produce a return on their capital, and secondly, to provide better roads in their area. With this in mind they would petition Parliament for an Act giving themselves powers to take over a defined section of the highway. Bear in mind that at this time, secure investments for wealth other than land were relatively few. In addition, Company Law was quite undeveloped and the trust created by Parliament was a ready means of forming a suitable legal entity to manage the road.

In all cases of turnpiking, initiative was local. This was the great age of laisser faire, and it was simply not thought part of a state's function to do much more than maintain law and order and conduct foreign policy. Consequently, Parliament did not decide which roads needed attention and impose a Turnpike Act. Local residents concerned in a particular road met, subscribed the funds to pay the legal charges to obtain an Act, and if their petition was successful became trustees. Naturally, improvement and development of a road system under such conditions was haphazard and depended on local soil types and traffic, availability of local materials for repairs and the resourcefulness of residents.

A Turnpike Act usually laid down how many Trustees were to be appointed, what qualifications they must possess, how much capital each must subscribe to the undertaking and their powers, including the tolls they were allowed to levy. An 18th century Act for Endon in Staffordshire states that prospective Trustees should be entitled to rents of at least £50 annually, have personal estate of £1000, or be heir apparent to a person with land yielding a yearly income of £100.

Apart from powers to erect gates and collect tolls at authorised levels, trustees could appoint new trustees, employ surveyors and collectors, and demand the old statute labour obligations, or their equivalent in money. They could also raise capital by mortgaging future tolls, and it was intended that this would be the main method of raising money for initial repair work. When income from the tolls had paid off the debt, it was intended that the road would revert to the parishes. Trusts were therfore set up for limited periods, usually twenty one years. In practice they rarely succeeded in paying off their debts and were renewed by Parliament as a matter of course.

There might be a great many trustees named in a Turnpike Act, in some cases well over a hundred. The first Evesham Turnpike Act of 1728 listed over one hundred and thirty names, many of them people with interests in different sections of the road. The list commenced with the nobility of the district and continued with gentry, professional people and clergy. Erasmus Darwin, grandfather of Charles Darwin, appeared on an 18th century Turnpike Trust in Lichfield. Trustees acted through a clerk who was usually a lawyer, a treasurer who was often a banker, and a surveyor whose qualifications throughout the 18th century were usually minimal. This was mainly because, whatever the Romans had known, 18th century Europe had very limited knowledge of how to build roads suitable for wheeled vehicles.

The turnpike surveyor was required to pay for labour and materials for initial repair or construction of a road at current rates. But in matters of upkeep they were soon given almost as many powers as parish surveyors, as well as having the backing of the powerful body of local trustees. From 1714 onwards the turnpike surveyor was given explicit power to exact the carrying out, under his own direction, of a proportion (usually a third) of the statute labour and team duties of the parishioners. He was also authorised to take gravel, stone, chalk or other materials from the common lands without payment, or from private ground simply on payment for incidental damages. Although never empowered to collect a money rate, the trusts were authorised to demand a lump sum from the parishes in lieu of statute labour.

At first the gates built by the trusts were watched by an employee from a wooden hut and the gates were often closed at night. But when it became clear that they were to be more than temporary, purpose built toll houses were built in key positions, usually at road junctions on the edges of towns. In Birmingham they stood on all major routes - Soho Road, Moseley Road, Bristol Road.

A toll house on the Dudley and Wolverhampton road still stands in Smethwick High Street. Another at The Angel junction in Sparkbrook controlled access to the Statford Road which had further gates at Acocks Green, Shirley and Henley in Arden. The gate at Cannon Hill let travellers onto the Pershore road leading to the Stirchley and West Heath gates.

Excellent examples of two toll houses on roads out of the same town can be seen near Halesowen. On the B4551 Bromsgrove road, some 400 yards from the roundabout at the A456 (Birmingham - Kidderminster) and at the top of Grange Hill, the somewhat altered toll house faces downhill. In the past it had pointed windows. On the Stourbridge Road is a pleasant, single storey circular ladies' hairdressers which only lightly disguises its origins. Another gate stood near the Kings Highway, Quinton.

In the early days of the system the wrong type of man seems to have been employed, usually at the low wage of 9 shillings per week. There were many complaints of the gates being locked,

Midland Toll Houses

Smethwick

Arrow, south of Alcester

Stourbridge Road, Halesowen

with the toll keeper either asleep and unable to be roused, drunk or missing.

Eventually practices improved, with the local Justices imposing fines on toll keepers and travellers under the General Turnpike Acts. But the main instrument of change was "toll farming". This involved the trustees letting out the collection of tolls annually to the highest bidder, usually through the local paper. The winner would pay the trustees a fixed amount and keep the tolls collected. An item in the *Worcestershire Journal* for 5th September 1754 reads:

> "This is to give Notice, that the Henley and Shirley-Street Toll GATES will be Lett, to the BEST BIDDERS by the Commissioners of the Turnpikes, who meet at the White Swan in Henley on Monday .... for that purpose. And also that a SURVEYOR is wanted to take care of the ROADS between Henley and Birmingham."

For some areas the names of successful contractors are known to us. One such was Thomas Parker, of Lane's End, Kenil-worth. He bid successfully for a number of years and put a toll keeper in the Bradnock's Marsh toll house in the town. Toll farming encouraged a more responsible type of toll keeper whose standard of living depended on how much he could collect at his gates over and above what he was paying the Trustees. As the system improved collectors began to receive a monthly wage as well as a rent free house. However there were abuses, as it was known for one man to bid successfully for several toll gates and employ others to man them.

Different trusts had their own styles, but toll houses were usually elegant, compact structures of brick or local stone, attractive as well as functional. Some were round, but most hexagonal or square, with a few built as half octagons, all des-igned so the windows faced every direction from which traffic might come. They were sometimes given wide protecting eaves, at least on the gateward side, so that the gate or "pike keeper" could have some shelter as he took tolls in wet weather. Interior fittings usually included a built in till, which in one case was ingeniously made part of the kitchen dresser.

Sometimes toll houses were not purpose built, but a structure used for toll gathering because of its strategic position on a particular road. Many such buildings, including some purpose built toll houses, became dwellings and show few traces of their former function.

Tolls were payable on a fixed scale of charges which varied a great deal through the turnpike era. They were also changed frequently by the individual trusts in response to various local pressures. Toll on the Birmingham to Edgehill turnpike (now Stratford Road) varied varied from 3d to 1 shilling for coaches, depending on the number of horses, and from 2d to 8d for carts. Farm animals were charged by the score, sheep at 5d, cattle 10d.

In 1726 under an Act for repairing roads into Worcester the following rates were fixed:

	s d
For every coach etc. drawn by 4 or more horses	1 0
For the like drawn by 1 or 2 horses	0 6

To prevent misuse of this system there were usually penalties for allowing traffic to pass over private land with the intention of avoiding tolls, quite a common practice among farmers with fields near a toll gate. It was also an offence for those who had paid a toll and acquired a ticket to sell it on to someone else. (Toll tickets were available for 24 hours). In a 1729 Act of the Lichfield Turnpike Trust, the fine for each of these offences was 12 shillings.

Local pressures had influence on the amount of tolls charged and on what kind of traffic was exempt. All trusts made their own regulations under their own and any relevant general Acts of Parliament. In Evesham for example, flour millers were granted freedom of access for their customers and for materials to repair their mills. In the First Staffordshire Turnpike Act of 1714 there were exemptions to placate local farmers, coal carriers and iron masters who might otherwise have opposed the Bill in Parliament. In the Ludlow Second Turnpike Act, early in the 19th century, persons exempt from paying toll included those:

"carrying any quantities of Stones, Bricks, Lime, Timber, Wood, Gravel or other materials for repairing the Roads, or the streets of the town of Ludlow, Cleobury Mortimer or Knighton,"

There were also general exemptions from toll which applied to most areas. These usually included carriages or people travelling on horseback on days of Parliamentary or County elections, agricultural traffic such as carts of dung or mold, and livestock being taken or driven to market, vehicles carrying people to church, soldiers on the march and all carriages and carts attending them, post horses carrying the mail, vehicles or horses carrying materials for the repair of roads in the parish and all pedestrians. Many Trusts charged double on Sundays and some applied a surcharge of 50% on all tolls between 31st October and 1st May.

The toll payable depended on the size of vehicle and the number of animals hauling it. However in the second half of the 18th century weight began to be taken into account, when it became clear that it affected the degree of damage to a road surface. Towns with frequent markets or fairs or producing merchandise had to install weighing machines or "engines". Here drivers of loaded wagons leaving town would have them weighed and receive a ticket, which they could produce at toll gates. This idea has much in common with the modern tax on heavy lorries.

The weighing "engines" were large timber structures, frequently out of order, which combined the functions of a crane and a steelyard, the vehicles being winched off the ground for weighing. In Birmingham in 1830 there were weighing machines at 103 Snow Hill and 15 Princip Street. In Evesham, the weighing machine stood outside the town hall facing Vine Street, and there are records of them in Upton upon Severn, Alcester and Henley in Arden, among other places.

The major problem with the weighing machine system was not unreliable machinery but the dishonesty of so many of the engine keepers. These men would agree with the wagoners to share the money saved by not declaring the full weight their vehicles, so defrauding the trusts of large sums of money.

Just as tolls were farmed, the rights to operate weighing machines were let annually. This was usually done by public auction, and as the rents were often two or three times the theoretical highest annual value of the weighing fees, it is obvious that fraud was practised on a large scale.

Another function of the turnpike trustees was to erect milestones or mileposts along their roads. The first appeared in 1663, the year of the first Turnpike Act, marking distances along the Dover Road. Each trust had its own style of stone or post which varied in different parts of the country, and even within the Midlands. Surviving examples show that some were wooden, some of iron, but mostly of stone with either a metal plaque showing the distance to the next two towns, or with the information carved into the stone.

Probably the earliest surviving road sign in the country is the "Cross Hands" signpost on Broadway Hill in the Cotswolds. This was a private guide post made of iron and provided by Nathaniel Izod of Chipping Campden in 1669. Local tradition has it that the iron spike was used to impale sheep stealers.

In Evesham the trustees favoured a big stone with a milage plaque and some can still be seen on roads leaving the town, though with one exception they are plaqueless. The person responsible for them in the 1930s and 40s asserts that they were removed soon after the outbreak of World War II to comply with Defence Regulations. Apparently it was felt that, like direction signs, they would help an invading enemy.

Many early milestones served both as milestone and mounting block, in some areas called upping stones. They are found most particularly across Dunsmore, south-east of Coventry. In the iron making districts of the Midlands, 19th Century cast iron milestones are still common, especially along main roads in Staffordshire. The Stratford upon Avon to Oxford turnpike had cast iron mile markers, some of which survive. These closely resemble a lampost without the lamp, having a fluted column with ornate foliated base.

The turnpike system reached the Midlands in one of the eight Acts passed in the 1706/7 Parliamentary session. It covered the road from Old Stratford, in Northamptonshire, to Dun-church, some 29 miles of the great road to the north-west. In 1713 Worcestershire obtained its first turnpike for the Droitwich to Worcester road. Two of the first three Stafford-shire Acts, those of 1714 and 1728, covered stretches of roads from London to Chester and Carlisle via Lichfield and Stone.

The first Turnpike Act to affect the Black Country was passed in May 1727, enabling tolls to be collected on the existing roads from Wednesbury to Brettel Lane on the outskirts of Stourbridge, via Great Bridge (Tipton) and Dudley. This linked coal producing areas to the east of the Sedgley - Northfield ridge with Birming-ham, and crossed the ridge at its lowest point at Dudley. To the west of this ridge, the turnpike crossed the sparsely populated Pensnett Chase to the glass producing areas around Stourbridge. From here, a road linked with the port of Bewdley on the River Severn.

*Miscellaneous milestones and
milepost near Newbold on Stour*

Important towns had their own concentration of roads. Because of the importance of the roads passing through Lichfield, a turnpike trust for their maintenance was set up comparatively early. The Lichfield Turnpike Trust received its first Act in 1729, and it was amended by Acts of 1744, 1755 and 1789. However, with the onset of the Industrial Revolution, it was Birmingham that became the main town of the Midlands and the focus for the region's most important road network.

The Birmingham - Stratford upon Avon - Edgehill route (the Stratford Road), and Birmingham - Warwick - Warmington route (the Warwick Road) were the first to be turnpiked in 1725/6. Birmingham to Bromsgrove (part of the Bristol Road) and Birmingham to Wednesbury (part of the Holyhead Road), were turnpiked in 1726/7, and Birmingham to Stonebridge (the modern Coventry Road) in 1744/5. The road from Spernall Ash just south of Studley to Digbeth (now Alcester Road) was turnpiked in 1766/7. The Pershore Road was built as a new turnpike in 1825.

In Hutton's *History of Birmingham* written in 1783, some of these roads are described critically. The Bromsgrove - Birmingham road was "extremely commodious for the first 4 (miles), but after is so confined that two horses cannot pass without danger". The Alcester Road was "rather too narrow, through desolate country", "those to Stratford and Warwick ... much used and much neglected."

Most Turnpike Acts applied to improve the existing roads and seldom to build new stretches. New works included part of the old Holyhead mail route around the Earl of Aylesford's park at Packington, part of the Banbury Road round Castle Park at Warwick, Pershore Road mentioned above, and part of Thomas Telford's Holyhead Road on either side of Coventry.

In the years 1751-1772 came what has been called "Turnpike Mania". Three hundred and eighty nine new trusts were set up, and there was even a popular demand for them in parts of the West Midlands. When in 1763 the Burslem Potters led by Josiah Wedgwood petitioned Parliament for a turnpike to bypass Newcastle under Lyme, Newcastle people counter petitioned for a road that did not go:

"only through small villages so that the same seems solely calculated to serve the interests of a few private persons."

In 1773 a General Turnpike Act opened the way for national economic expansion by extending arrangements for money for road repairs to be collected by taxation, and drew attention to the rank impossibility of maintaining through routes while local variations continued. The lawmakers had finally realised that instead of trying to adapt traffic to the roads, the roads must be adapted to the traffic.

A further function of the Turnpike Trusts was construction and maintenance of bridges. At a public meeting on the 17th January 1787 it was resolved that the old bridge at Deritend, Birmingham be replaced. To pay for this the bridge had to be turnpiked, and the Bridge Act was obtained in 1788.

To prevent flooding of the lower part of Digbeth in heavy rain, the course of the River Rea was recut, widened and deepened by some 30 feet below Bradford Street. Tolls charged on the new bridge included 2d for every four wheeled carriage and 1/2d for every horse not drawing. There was also a fine of 40 shillings for attempting to cross without paying.

In notice appeared in *Aris's Birmingham Gazette* of Monday 3rd July 1826 about the bridge and other nearby toll gates:

> "The toll at Deritend bridge turnpike gate and gates erected in Bradford Street, Cheapside, Moseley Street, Watery Lane and Fazeley Street to be let by tender on Thursday 3rd August at the Public Office in Birmingham. Tolls are now let for £525."

The late 18th century was a time of rapid expansion in the regional economy of the Midlands, and after the 1770s turnpike improvements were supplemented by a series of roads created by various Enclosure Acts. In return for being allowed to enclose previously common or public land for their own use, landowners were obliged to create public roads across their new holdings. These supplied the vital network of local roads linking specific smaller villages and industrial premises with the turnpikes and canals. However, enclosures were then and always had been, extremely unpopular with much of the population, despite their occasional necessity.

Gradually, with the expansion of industry and generally better paid work to be found in towns, the countryside began to depopulate. A new social conflict broke out between the gentry and those who realised that, if a rapidly increasing population was to be fed, agriculture would need to be organised on industrial lines and the extensive areas of unused land brought into production. Waste land must therefore be enclosed and more intensive methods of cultivation encouraged. Enclosures were to change the rural landscape as drastically as mechanization later changed the urban, with marshes drained, commons enclosed, scrub cleared and woodland felled.

Under the Enclosure Acts the landscape was divided into regular shaped plots crossed by straight roads, giving the familiar English, chequerboard landscape. Where the old roads ran around trees and ponds, often following ancient cattle trails, the new ones were bold and direct. A glance at any road map shows the pattern that emerged over much of the wide Midland belt that was fast becoming the workshop of England.

Within a couple of generations great areas of the Midlands took on a new look and new infrastructure. Amongst other things, it allowed long distance coaches to pass through the heavily populated counties speedily and safely. It brought many towns in the region within reach of through routes, giving the area a great advantage for expanding trade.

A considerable proportion of land affected by enclosures was set aside for these public roads. In Kingswinford manor alone, 157 acres were designated for roads in the awards for Ashwood Hay and Pensnett Chase. Main roads such as those between Dudley and Stourbridge, or Stourbridge and Kidderminster and the Wolverhampton turnpike at Wall Heath, were to be 60 feet wide excluding ditches, somewhat wider than the present roads.

These main highways would allow plenty of space for wheeled vehicles to pass and lessen the likelihood of impassable rutted sections. In 1781 the Court Leet Rolls record that the road from Wordsley to Kingswinford near Dudley was wide enough for only one vehicle. It was improved as part of the main road from Stourbridge to the Wolverhampton turnpike by the Pensnett Chase Enclosure Award.

A second category of roads was laid down with a width of 40 feet. Provision was also made for bridle roads 20-30 feet wide and public footpaths and cattle paths varying in width from 6 to 20 feet.

These widths were common in the enclosure awards of most areas and intended to give space to manoeuvre around particularly bad patches of road. They created the wide grass verges bordering so many roads today. Where the award required a new road it was usually built straight to reduce expense. In some areas enclosure roads replaced old, winding lanes but took a slightly different route and in some cases bypassed ancient settlements.

It must not be forgotten that throughout the turnpike era, local or minor roads remained the responsibility of the parishes. This added up to many thousands of miles of roads, including several important through routes.

For much of the 18th century, the fact that a road was turnpiked did not necessarily mean that it had been much improved. Many roads were still poor and contemporary observers such as Hutton remarked on the difficulty of road travel.

In Shropshire the roads seem to have been particularly hazardous. In 1762 John Wesley preached in Shrewsbury, and a friend volunteered to send him and his companion on to Wem in a post chaise. But the road was so bad that the chaise stuck fast and the horses broke their harness trying to pull it out. Archdeacon Plymley wrote of Stoke St Milborough, in 1793:

"being within the franchise of Wenlock the inhabitants must resort thither along a very bad road of 15 miles for the purpose of justice

"And in the neighbouring parish of Clee St. Margaret - the roads are narrow and deep during winter .. most ..are impassable for horses even in summer."

Per Kalm, a Swedish cleric passing through the Midlands in the 1740s, noted that the;

"roads are so deep seems to have come from this ... very large wagons are used with many horses in front, on which wagons a very heavy load is laid."

It was these wagons, he surmised, that had "eaten down into the ground" and deepened the road.

Despite these inadequacies, the turnpike roads were usually an improvement on what had gone before. Journey times were cut and freight rates lowered, because the expense of tolls was more than balanced by reduction in the number of horses required to pull heavy loads. In 1777 in Matthew Pickford was advertising his "flying wagons" which took only four and a half days to travel from Manchester to London.

Much more alarming than the complaints against road conditions were those levelled against the turnpike system itself. Throughout the 18th century many toll gates were destroyed by angry citizens. The main complainants were usually local farmers who felt they were being unjustly treated as they not only had to pay tolls, but give statute labour or team duty in their own parishes.

Often in the early years of the system, financial mismanagement by trusts had prevented any obvious improvement in the road network, and this led to widespread disillusionment. Though many avoided the tolls completely by taking different routes, others protested more directly. As early as 1732, a riotous armed mob marched into Hereford threatening to destroy the turnpikes and murder the "pikemen", with the trustees who employed them.

Even so, as the system developed there were clear improvements, and though there never was widespread acceptance, by the early 19th century views seemed to be changing. William Pitt, in his *General View of Agriculture in the County of Worcestershire,* wrote in 1813:

> "toll gates in Worcestershire are neither numerous nor extravagant in their tolls; a good deal of the heavy traffic being taken off them by the navigable rivers and canals."

He gave much credit for the improvement of the country roads to Lord Coventry, who became one of the Evesham trustees. He owned large estates on the Broadway Hills and at Earls Croome near Upton upon Severn, and built that strange landmark, the Broadway Tower, at the highest point to give him a view over his entire estate. Lord Coventry put a lot of money into turnpikes to ensure comfortable travel between his estates.

During the 1820s and 1830s corresponding with the golden age of coaching, turnpike trusts were responsible for around 25,000 miles of roads in England and Wales. This was a greater route mileage than the railway network at its most comprehensive. The period 1824-6 were boom years for road speculation and saw the creation of fifty new trusts. By 1835 twenty two trusts in Worcestershire controlled 758 miles of road, incurring an expenditure of £2,236 and producing an income of £3,785.

In Lichfield the turnpike trust's business expanded steadily as traffic increased on Watling Street from London, or through Stoney Stratford and Coleshill. The rent of the Branston toll gate in the City, went up from £59 in 1816 to £90 in 1833.

In 1835 the General Turnpike Act abolished the ancient duty of statute labour under the 1555 Act. All the restrictive and contradictory regulations concerning wheel widths in relation to lines of draught were abolished, and the modern system of using salaried officials and labour hired at the market rate was established. Unfortunately and more important, the administrative units charged with road repairs were left unchanged in function or size. The Act left some 15,000 "highway parishes", half of them containing fewer than fifty families, responsible for spending more at £1,000,000 a year of maintenance of 104,700 miles of road.

In addition to these parishes there were by 1838 1,116 Turnpike Trusts maintaining 22,000 miles of road, employing 3,555 treasurers, clerks and surveyors and 20,000 toll collectors. Their toll receipts from 7,796 gates and side bars amounted to £1,458,000 of which about £51 was spent on each mile of road, the rest being partly used to service some £7,000,000 of funded debt, or wasted through fraud and inefficiency. In contrast the 104,700 miles of parish roads had only £11 spent on each mile.

An ominous sign of the toll paying public's unrest at such an uneven and unfair system came in 1842-3 with the so called "Rebecca Riots" in South Wales. The name derived from a passage in Genesis 24:60, in which Isaac's wife is promised that her descendants will "possess the gate of those which hate them". Calling themselves Rebecca and her children, and with leaders dressed in women's clothes, the rioters smashed and burnt turnpike gates and toll houses. Their actions may have been extreme, but the authorities seem to have been conscious of the injustices of the turnpike system and those caught were treated leniently.

The turnpike system was intended to provide for everyone to contribute to the maintenance of roads in proportion to the use they made of them. But its real weakness was that it relied on private enterprise for what eventually would have to become a national responsibility. It worked so unevenly that it satisfied neither those saw it as abandonment of the idea of free travel on the highways, nor those who resented having to pay to use their own local roads. In practice it included the additional weakness that the tolls collected in rural areas, where the worst roads were found, could never raise the money necessary to achieve the standards expected for coach travel.

Despite their many shortcomings, the turnpike trusts did some useful work which perhaps could not have been done by any other means given the resources and attitudes prevalent in 18th century England. They also helped make possible the remarkable speeds and regularity of road travel in the heyday of the coaching era. Their role in passenger transport was not really as important as the part they played in the Industrial Revolution. Improved roads allowed wheeled goods vehicles, like Matthew Pickford's wagons, to reach places formerly inacessible through the quagmires.

The network provided by these turnpike roads remained the basis of the main road system in England and Wales until the coming of the motorways and other new roads in the middle of the 20th century. Even today many main roads follow former turnpike routes.

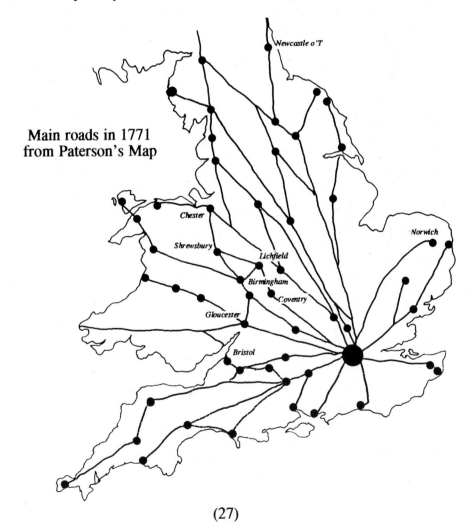

Main roads in 1771 from Paterson's Map

The Road Builders

The turnpike had provided a financial basis for maintaining roads used by long distance traffic, but it achieved little before 1800 to improve methods of construction and maintenance. Improvements that occurred were slow to come and soon overtaken by increasing traffic. Few people understood that road management was a skilled occupation, and that road surveyors and builders should be trained in their craft.

Methods of road construction varied throughout the country. In south-east England ditches were usually dug on either side of the road, excavated earth was piled onto it and covered with gravel. In the north a deep trench was dug the full width of the road, filled with large stones and roughly surfaced with smaller ones. Both types of road easily became waterlogged.

In the Midlands, tolls on the Birmingham to Edgehill turnpike were increased by half in 1770-1 to pay for reconstruction from bedrock. The work was spread over several decades, and involved straightening sharp bends, reducing steep gradients, and making new stretches of road where the old ways were particularly bad. Graded layers of broken stone were rolled down to provide a firm, smooth surface, with fine gravel placed on top.

In general the 18th century roadmaker's equipment consisted of a pick, a stout wooden rake, a shovel, a basket and sometimes a wheelbarrow. Some villages also kept the "road plough", drawn by eight or more horses. Every spring it was used to restore the parish roads by ploughing them and throwing the furrows towards the centre. The furrows were then flattened by harrowing and the roads presumed ready for summer traffic.

Such dirt roads became waterlogged and useless after heavy or prolonged rain. An improvement found on heavily used routes was to lay a causeway, 2 to 4 feet wide along the centre or near side of the road. This paved way was raised above the general level of the road, and as wheeled vehicles were still thought of as intruders, many parishes separated the "causey" from the soft road by a line of upright posts.

When suitable stone was available it was used in abundance, but to little effect. The roads were usually dug unnecessarily deep, and the resultant trench filled up with ungraded stones to a depth of 3 feet or more. This was then topped with gravel, unwashed and unadulterated with mud and clay. Usually the surfaces were so steeply cambered that wheeled traffic was severely impeded.

The main problem with these 18th century roads was that they absorbed water, which was aggravated by the use of water to maintain them. Road surfaces were made slightly concave, and by blocking culverts and temporarily diverting streams into the roadway, mud and debris was washed to the lowest point, where it would be cleared by men with spades. With the increased traffic of heavily laden wagons, this resulted in "hollow ways" or "concave roads". During prolonged rain they became brooks. Where they had sufficient "bottoming", this system worked well enough for narrow lanes, provided the disadvantage was overlooked that the roadway gradually sank between the adjacent fields. This would go on until, as Edgeworth wrote in 1817:

> "... the stag, the hounds and the huntsmen had been known to leap over a loaded wagon in a hollow way without any obstruction from the vehicle."

The holloways, now waterproofed and no longer concave, are still with us. We have Holloway Head leading west from Horsefair, Birmingham, Bell Holloway in Northfield - a very clear example, and Holloway Bank in West Bromwich.

Much of the limited progress in road making techniques in the 18th century has to be credited to a few individuals among the justices and trustees of the turnpike trusts. These were people who took their appointments more seriously than the majority, and paid as much attention to their duties as highway administrators as they did to their estates.

One progressive was the Reverend Henry Homer, who became a trustee of the two roads meeting at Ryton on Dunsmore just southeast of Coventry. One is now the A45 from Dunchurch (south of Rugby) which ran via Coventry to Stonebridge, and the other is now the A423 from Ryton to Banbury. In 1767 he published a shilling pamphlet - *An Enquiry into the Means of Preserving and Improving the Public Roads of this Kingdom*. In it he stated:

> "two great objectives to kept in View ... are to support them [the roads] in convenient State for Use, and to effect them with as small Expense as possible, of Materials."

This should be done, he said, by guarding roads against unnecess-ary damage, by limiting weights of vehicles, regulating vehicle construction and regulating the usage of roads. Such ideas paved the way for more important changes in road management and construction which were to begin at the end of the century.

During the late 18th, and early 19th century, significant progress in road construction began to be made due mainly to the work of three men, who set precedents for the rest of the world.

John Metcalf (1717-1810) of Knaresborough in Yorkshire (or "Blind Jack"- he lost his sight as a child), had been a musician, soldier, fish dealer. pedlar, horse dealer and had his own carrier business for which he often used to drive the wagons. Metcalf produced an improved road by using a firm foundation covered with road stone, which produced an arched surface to throw off rainwater into ditches. He first used this technique in 1765 on a turnpike road in Yorkshire, eventually extending it to 180 miles of turnpike in that county. Metcalf was the pioneer whose work was the forerunner of the more extensive improvements early the next century by Telford and Macadam.

John Loudon Macadam (1756-1836) was a Scotsman who had spent several years in America, Europe and Scandinavia and was acquainted with many different road making methods. Macadam postulated that, provided the road surface was made waterproof by the attrition and compaction of properly graded stones, a thickness of 6 to 10 inches should be enough, and the natural soil beneath would carry any weight likely to pass over it. Much of his work was concerned with re-making existing roads, but his approach worked as well on new sections.

By 1811 he was giving evidence to the House of Commons Select Committee on highways and turnpike roads in England and Wales. In 1816, aged 60, he was appointed surveyor to the Bristol Turn-pike Trust, of which he was already a trustee. This put him in charge of around 149 miles of road, on which to put his theories into practice. Much of Macadam's fame rested on the economy of his system and the employment it gave to women, children, and men too old or feeble for heavy physical work. His contrib-ution to road construction was immense, and his name put the "mac" into tarmac (in full - tarmacadam).

Thomas Telford (1757-1834) was the son of a Dumfriesshire shepherd, but was born and learned his trade in Eksdale as a journeyman mason, where he built bridges over the fast flowing streams of the Lake District, and later Scotland. Simply put, Telford's method of road building was to lay a 6 inch layer of broken stones on a foundation of larger ones and surface it with gravel, taking care that the stones were properly pitched and cambered for drainage. His roads were, almost for the first time, designed with the wheeled vehicle in mind, with gradients and curves made as easy as possible.

In contrast to his contemporary, Macadam can be seen as an amateur working by common sense and observation. Telford was one of the first to qualify for the title of professional civil engineer in the modern sense. He was also one of the first engineers to master the technique of using iron on a large scale, and built scores of bridges exhibiting new modes of design and construction. Many are still in use, ranging from simple, single span, stone arches over small streams, to such masterpieces as the Menai Suspension Bridge in North Wales which opened in January 1826.

Probably Telford's greatest achievement was the Holyhead Road (from London). Originally the mail coach route from London had been via Chester and the North Wales coast, with ferry crossings at the Conwy Estuary and the Menai Strait. A turnpike road built around 1804 through North Wales from Shrewsbury to Bangor avoided the Conwy crossing, and mail coaches were diverted onto it. But it was a steep, narrow and dangerous road; on the western approach to its summit over 1000 feet above sea level near Llyn Ogwen, it became as narrow as 15 feet and as steep as 1 in 13. Mainly because of the accidents suffered by Irish MPs travelling to London, the government were forced to employ Telford to survey it, and his report was published in 1811.

Nothing was done until 1815 when the cause was taken up by Henry Parnell, MP for Queen's County. In that same year the Holyhead Road Commission was set up by Parliament with Telford as engineer, and work continued under his direction for fifteen years.

The alignment of the Holyhead Road is typical of a road built for horse drawn coaches. Steep hills were eliminated as they slowed the horses to an unsatisfactory walk uphill, and were dangerous to descend. Gradients were 1 in 22 1/2, an easy trotting slope for a coach horse. Through the Nant Ffrancon pass with its 1000 feet summit, the road has a ruling gradient of 1 in 22. Coach horses would not exceed 15 or 16 miles per hour at very best, so the road and especially the bends are laid for speeds of this sort.

The Holyhead Road was made 30 feet wide, and used techniques developed from the Highland, Glasgow and Carlisle Road, such as retaining walls, breastworks, masonry bridges, good drainage. In 1815 a large and handsome cast iron bridge was built to carry the road across the River Conwy at Betws y Coed, one of the first of its type. Perhaps the main consequence of this vast undertaking was the improvement in the speed and reliability of stagecoaches, a vital contribution to the golden age of coaching which was began just a few years later.

The road making techniques used by Metcalf, Macadam and Telford were essentially the same, and an intruiging question remains about their origins. We could attribute them to a coupling of common sense with some knowledge of Roman methods and leave it at that, were it not for their immediate predecessors. Following the Jacobite Rebellion of 1715, General Wade supervised the building of some 250 miles of military roads in the Scottish Highlands in the years after 1725. After the second uprising in 1745 another 800 miles of roads were laid under Major Caulfield. These roads were largely built by troops, who first cut a road bed and heaped the spoil to form banks. Gravel was then built up in layers using smaller materials near the urface. Water was carried off through open, stone lined cross drains, and later culverts. They were good roads in the sense that they were well laid, drained and surfaced, but bad roads in that they served no other than a military purpose. Once they were no longer required for this function they could not promote trade where none existed, and the gradients were often uneccessarily steep. They remain as rural tracks used mainly by walkers and farmers.

These roads were started when Blind Jack Metcalf was a baby and long before Macadam or Telford were born. The thoroughness and sufficiency of the technique suggests that Wade was drawing upon more than experimental experience; it suggests long practice and a clear understanding of the need for drainage and consolidation which must surely reach back into at least the 17th century. Somewhere people knew how to build good roads and I have, for the time being, left the question there.

"If God Permit"
Dawn of the Coaching Age

The coach probably takes its name from the small town of Kocs
in Hungary, where four wheeled passenger vehicles were built, from
the late Middle Ages. The first coach known in England was built
for the Earl of Rutland by Walter Rippon, who also made a "hollow
turning coach" for Queen Mary. Twenty years later, he was responsible for a "chariot throne", in which Queen Elizabeth travelled
to St Paul's Cathedral in great ceremony to attend a public
thanksgiving for the defeat of the Armada.

The historian John Stowe (1526 - 1605) mentions William Bonnen,
Queen Elizabeth's coachman, who brought an early Dutch coach to
Britain in the 1560s. Stowe describes reaction to it, presum-
ably by country people:

> "...a coach was a strange monster in those days, and the
> site of them put both horses and man into amazement; some
> said it was a great crab-shell brought out of China, and
> some imagined it to be one of the Pagan Temples in which
> the Cannibals adored the devil."

Coaches were extremely cumbersome and awkward things in
the early 17th century, often drawn by as many as ten or twelve
horses. According to one 19th century source, so called "long-
waggons" or "machines", "covered with matting and curtains"
to protect passengers, ran between London and Canterbury and
probably other large towns, as early as 1605.

But evidence for the first known stagecoach comes some years
later. This was the service running from London to St Albans in
1637. Entries such as "the waggon or coach of Hertford" and "the
waggon or coach of Hatfield", in Taylor's *Carrier's Cosmography*
of 1637 may be references to early stagecoaches; it is not certain.

The first stagecoach run to involve the Midlands was from London
to Chester, via Coventry, Lichfield and Stone, which was certainly
in operation by 1659. Macaulay, in his *History of England* (1849),
contends that it was started on 6th April 1657, the 182 mile journey
taking five days. He adds that three men, William Dunstan, Henry
Earle, and William Fowler, staked their possessions on the success
of the enterprise. Whatever the exact starting date, this service was
maintained except during the Plague Year of 1665/6 until the
coming of the railways in the 1830s.

As the 17th century progressed, more and more large towns were linked to London by the stagecoach system. A Birmingham coach was first mentioned by Sir William Dugdale in his diary of 1679. By 1688 there were stagecoaches running from London to eighty eight different towns, and by 1705 they had increased to 180.

However, the stagecoach did not become widely popular for many years and was even considered effeminate by many 17th century people. Those who could afford it travelled on horseback (a good horse cost the equivalent of 2-3 years wages for a labourer), as did Samuel Johnson and his bride on their wedding journey to Derby.

Stratford upon Avon,

Two Days Stage-Coach to *London*,

Begins *Tuefday*, *April* the 3d. 1705.

GOes from the *Swan* Inn in *Stratford* every *Tuefday*, through *Wellsbourn* by *Compton-Verney* and *Kington*, through *Banbury* to *Alisbury*, and to the *Bell* Inn in *Holborn* ; and Returns from thence every *Friday*, by and through the fame Places to the *Swan-* Inn in *Stratford*, fetting out exactly at Four of the Clock in the Morning.

Performed, (if God permit) by { *Charles Stokes,* AND *Daniel Style.*

And at *Banbury*, *Alisbury*, or *Stratford*, at a Day's Warning, you may be furnifhed with a good Coach, Chariot, Calafh, Mourning Coach, Herfe, Velvet Pall, Cloaks, Flambeaux, and Torches, at Reafonable Rates.

⁎⁎ *Banbury* Stage-Coach, Goes *Mundays* and *Fridays*; and Returns from the *Black-Bull* Inn in *Holborn*, *Tuefdays* and *Saturdays*, in One Day.

Some people were decidedly against this new form of travel. The writer of a pamphlet printed in the *Harleian Miscellany* entitled *The Grand Concern of England*, pronounced coaches to be:

> "one of the greatest mischiefs that have happened in late years to the kingdom." [He blamed them for] "destroying the breed of good horses...and making men careless of attending to good horsemanship...hindering the breed of watermen , who are the nursery for seamen ...[and] lessening his Majesty's revenue."

A similar protest came from an early 17th century "waterman", who had his own remedy for the situation:

> "coaches and Sedans, they deserve both to be throwne into the Thames, and but for stopping the Channell, I would they were."

Coaches were much disliked by other road users. They became known as "hellcarts" because of the space they took up, with drivers demanding the right of way for their upper class passengers. Nevertheless, some contemporary writers approved of these new coaches. In *The Present State of England* (1669) Edward Chamberlayne wrote of their advantages:

> "wherein one may be transported to any place sheltered from foul weather and foul ways, free from endangering of one's health and one's body by hard jogging or over violent motion on horseback; and this not only at the low price of about a shilling for every five miles, but with such velocity and speed in an hour as the foreign post can make but in one day.

Travel at this time was expensive and usually cumbersome. Few of the artisan and labouring classes took longer journeys than from one neighbouring town to another. Even in a large town such as Birmingham, probably few people knew what the sea or mountains looked like except from pictures. But at least the facilities were there and no doubt influenced the town to make local improvements and allowed for ideas to filter from the metropolis. At this time Birmingham was isolated from other towns by lack of navigable waterways, and there is no doubt that without the coach link with other great centres of industry and civilisation, it would not have made such rapid progress in industry and commerce.

In 1745 Birmingham is described in *England's Gazetteer* as :

"a large, well-built, and populous town, noted for the
most ingenious artificers in boxes, buckles, buttons and
other iron and steel wares, wherein such multitudes of
people are employed that they are sent all over Europe;
and here is a continual noise of hammers, anvils, and
files."

Many early stagecoaches were discarded private coaches, just as
some stagecoaches became private coaches in the mid 19th century.
Some must have been of obsolete design. In *Tales of an Antiquary*
published in the late 1820s, the writer describes the construction
of the coaches on the road in his youth:

"dull black leather" [with] "four oval windows, with heavy
red wooden frames, and green stuff or leather curtains."
[On the doors were written, in large letters] "the names
of the places whence the coach started, and whither it
went". [These were displayed, he says] "in quaint and
antique language."

The shape of the vehicles varied. Some were like a "distiller's
vat", others resembled a "violin-cello case...the most fashionable
form." At the back of the coach there was an

"immense basket, stretching far and wide beyond the body,
to which it was attached by iron bars or supports passing
beneath it." [The wheels were] "large, massive, ill-formed,
and usually of red colour".

Journeys in these early coaches were most uncomfortable because
they were unsprung. Leaf springs were introduced in the mid 17th
century, but not as part of any modern type of suspension. They
were used in combination with the leather braces which slung a
coach body from four upright posts on the undercarriage. Gradually
they were replaced by springs which evolved in the 19th century
into upright C-springs.

Several types of brakes were introduced from the late 17th century
but very few were of much use. The most reliable was the skidpan
or drag-shoe. This was an iron wedge or plate with a hollow centre
clamped to the near rearside wheel on downwards slopes. During
the first half of the 19th century both hand and pedal brakes were
introduced, followed by a manually operated screw brake. The
only stagecoach we have traced in the Midlands, in Birmingham

Museum and Art Gallery, was a late type. Ratchet hand levers beside front and rear nearside seats applied two shoes to the front and two to the back of the rear wheel.

The main passenger compartment of an 18th century coach usually seated between four and six people, while others stood or crouched in the basket on the back. Most coaches carried large amounts of luggage and parcels in vast boots underneath or at the rear. Some parcels and items such as game birds and turkeys were often hung on lamp brackets.

Around 1790 a number of constructional changes were made to stagecoaches, such as the driver's seat and the boot being built into the body. These led to the familiar design which was to last almost unchanged until the end of the 19th century.

The trade of coach and carriage building eventually employed many craftsmen and highly skilled workers, ranging from heraldic painters to body makers, wheelwrights and lamp makers. Although most of the parts were originally made under the same roof, from the mid 18th century there was a increasing specialisation. This led to many contracts for making fittings, including axles, springs and brakes. Most coach lamps, square or round, were originally lit by beeswax candles, and later by oil or battery lamps. Candles were the most reliable and much cleaner than oil lamps.

In the early coaches the coachman was seated, not on the slung portion of the vehicle, but on a bench or box fixed between the upright standards. This made four in hand driving impossible, so when more than two horses were used the leaders had to be controlled by a mounted groom or postillion. He usually rode the nearside leader, using his whip on its offside companion.

The reason why traffic in Britain came to drive on the left is that the majority of people are naturally right handed, and a coachman driving a British team or pair sat on the right of the box when this was shared with a groom or footman.

A coachman needed great stamina and skill, and there was no greater test than taking a heavy coach, sometimes weighing three tonnes or more, down a steep hill. At the top he stopped for the guard to to tie the drag shoe onto one of the rear wheels. Great strength was still needed by the two "wheelers" (horses nearest the coach) to hold it back, or it might run out of control and turn over. Some of the worst accidents happened when a coach-man trying to keep time was too impatient to stop and apply the brake at the top of every steep hill. Ascending hills was usually a considerable problem, and passengers often had to walk.

Shortly after the uncertainties of very early coach travel in the mid 17th century, attempts were made to run a "Flying Coach". At first this was attempted by using six horses and arranging relays to improve on the slow journey times. There were services between London and Oxford (1669), London and Cambridge (1671), London and Worcester (probably 1681), and no doubt other places. However, improvements were not achieved by going faster, but by starting very early in the morning and going on for what was usually advertised as twelve hours, but actually meant thirteen or fourteen. The terms "Flying Coach" or "Flying Machine" did not really catch on until many years later when they came into more general use in the 1740s.

Birmingham had enjoyed direct communication with London by stagecoach, however infrequent, since at least 1679. Increasing demand in the first half of the 18th century led to the first well documented regular service between the two cities, which was put on by Nicholas Rothwell of Warwick in 1731. When it started on 24th May, Rothwell promised that the journey would be performed in "Two Days and a half... if God permit". It was to set out from the Swan Inn, High Street, Birmingham on Mondays at 6 o'clock in the morning and the fare was 12 shillings. This service was followed by a *Flying Coach* in 1742, and an *Improved Birmingham Coach* in 1758.

In *Leafy Warwickshire* by George Morley published in 1895, there is mention of another early Birmingham coach called *The Fly*. He states that as early as 1700, this service ran from Birmingham to London on Monday of each week. It reached the City "after four days hard travelling".

A Stratford upon Avon to London coach started on 3rd April 1705 from The Swan Inn, Stratford, "exactly at Four of the Clock in the Morning." It was again, "Performed if God permit", this being the stagecoach proprietors' insurance against misfortune in these early days.

Titles given to stagecoaches could be misleading. A *Flying Coach, Diligence*, or *Accommodation* did not necessarily deliver to the traveller the facility implied. The *Diligence* was a coach carrying only three passengers on the Shrewsbury to London road. Competing with two other coaches, it travelled fastest at the lowest fare, but demand was poor and it was withdrawn. The

original coach had been fast and light, but the name later appeared on many vehicles, some carrying as many as eight people.

"Post" coaches and "Fast Post" coaches offering swifter travel
than ordinary stagecoaches were common in many towns from the
second half of the 18th century. By 1783 Edward Hart was running
the *Old Original London Post Coach* from The Swan, High Street,
Birmingham. The journey took just sixteen hours and the fare was
£1.12. 6d. Hart also offered a *Commodious Light Coach* to London
at a slightly more modest £1. 6s. In the same year Francis Piper
was running a *Post Coach* to Walsall and Wolverhampton, and *Light*
coaches to London, Manchester, Coventry and Kidderminster from
The Castle Inn, High Street. Mary Wells who kept The Chain, Bull
Street, ran a *Diligence* to Atherstone, and Ann Dunn of the George
Inn, Digbeth, put on coaches to Worcester, Shrewsbury and London.
There was also *A New and Elegant Post Coach* through Coventry to
London from The Dog Inn, Spiceal Street, Birmingham and many
more besides.

Whilst the names of stagecoaches might not reflect what type of
vehicle they were, they often did reflect current social or political topics. When ballooning first caught the public imagination
in the 1780s there soon appeared a number of *Balloon* coaches.
"Baloon Coach removed" stated an advertisement in *Aris's Birmingham Gazette* in August 1790, and there were many more even
after the first excitement had died down.

Coaches named after celebrated military figures and their vict-
ories on the battlefield proliferated. In 1805 we find *Nelsons*,
Lord Nelsons and *Trafalgars*. Royalty was patronised, and in an
August 1792 issue of *Aris's*, we read of *"The Royal Charlotte"*
running to London every night at 10.30. Many of the proprietors'
advertisments claimed the advantages of steel springs, and quicker
times were popular.

Coach travel was never cheap, and fares rose fairly steeply all
through the 18th century. From an average of just over 2d (just
under 1p) a mile in 1750, they increased to 4 1/2d (2.75p) per
mile in 1808. A copy of *The Times* newspaper cost 3d (1.25p) in
1785 and 6 1/2d (2.75p) in 1809. On longer journeys it was usual
to pay half the fare in advance, with the clerk entering the passengers' names and details in a huge ledger. Children on the lap
were usually half price, as were passengers who sat outside on
top of the coach. Travelling here could be extremely perilous, a
strong grip was needed since falling asleep could prove fatal,
hence the expression "to drop off".

Each passenger was allowed a certain weight of luggage, usually around 14 pounds. Stagecoach proprietors also stressed that they were not accountable for "Money, Bank Notes, Plate, Jewels &c. above the value of 5 pounds unless entered as such". Guards often accompanied coaches and this fact was always mentioned in advertisements. Etiquette at the time was such that no passenger without a hat was allowed to travel in or on a stagecoach.

In the early 18th century people would be pleased enough if a coach could manage 25 miles in a day. The average was probably 29 to 30 miles which, assuming an eight hour day, meant a speed of around 3.5 miles an hour. This would have been faster than a carrier's wagon but not as quick as horseback. By the 1760s coach speeds had increased and an average of 6 miles an hour was common. This coincided with a general improvement in coaches which had developed so far that it was possible to read a book while travelling.

By 1775 there were around four hundred registered stagecoaches on the road and the system seemed to be working tolerably well. Even so, the design of the vehicles and reliability of services were far from satisfactory. There were many complaints from passengers of uncomfortable journeys, unreliable and ignorant coachmen, theft and of course, highway robbery.

Down the hill on a frosty morning

The Highwayman

The English highwayman is inextricably mixed with myth and legend. The actual facts seem rather mundane compared with popular notions of daring, moonlit stagecoach hold ups by a masked hero on a jet black steed.

The highwayman became more active as road traffic increased, his (or very occasionally, her) heyday being from the mid 17th century, up until the mid 18th. Despite Macauley's quote - "he held an aristocratic position in the community of thieves", most highwaymen were unheroic villains who attacked lone travellers, and occasionally coaches, near London. Stories of the highwayman as a kind of Robin Hood, robbing the rich to help the poor, are almost entirely fictitious. The fruits of his crimes were more like to be enjoyed by himself.

Careers as highwaymen were in some cases small but significant parts of the lives of these men, with the remainder often devoted to more honest pursuits. There are also examples of the dissipated sons of aristocracy turning to highway robbery to pay off drinking and gambling debts.

Most highwaymen probably mixed robbery with other crimes such as burglary, poaching, smuggling and horse stealing, as did Dick Turpin. Due to the nature of the business, highwaymen usually lived a wandering life, constantly on the move to evade capture. Under such conditions their life expectancy in the role was short, probably a year or two at the most, and often much less.

Footpads, or thieves who robbed travellers on foot rather than on horseback, had been on the roads long before the stagecoach and the highwayman. The advantages of a horse for a quick escape must have prompted many footpads to acquired one and become highwaymen. Others did not, and the footpad continued to be a menace to the traveller well into the 18th century and beyond.

Every highway had its robbery black spots. Epping Forest, Hampstead Heath and Hounslow Heath were the worst. In the Midlands the main road from Birmingham to Warwick was among the most dangerous, while the Birmingham to Coventry route and the Chester Road around Sutton Coldfield had bad reputations.

These places were often associated with particular highwaymen. In Epping Forest it was Dick Turpin, and on Hounslow Heath, James Maclaine, son of a Presbyterian minister. Apparently, Maclaine was one of the "great gentlemen highwaymen" about which so much has been written. He followed the tradition of the infamous Claude Duval, a Frenchman who came to England in the service of the Duke of Richmond. Duval was so popular with the ladies that while he was awaiting execution in 1670, so many females of high rank pleaded for his life that only the judge's threat to resign if Duval did not hang prevented him being pardoned.

The most famous highwayman of all was certainly Dick Turpin. A farmers son born in Essex in 1705, be became involved with various criminal activities including cattle stealing and robbing smugglers off the Easy Anglian coast, sometimes posing as a Revenue Officer. He later joined a gang of deer stealers in Epping Forest who smuggled the venison for sale to London concealed under wagon loads of vegetables. Now known as "Gregory's Gang" they acquired fame for burglaries on the north-eastern outskirts of London. But when three of them were caught and hung the gang dispersed.

Turpin turned to highway robbery in partnership with a Birmingham highwayman called Tom King, who was born in Sutton Coldfield at a farmhouse between Sutton Park and Stonnall. Though Turpin and King are thought to have operated in many different areas, including Watling Street between Nuneaton and Leicester, their base of operations was a cave in Epping Forest. Food and supplies were apparently brought to them by Turpin's legal wife. One story goes that the landlord of the Green Man at Epping apprehended Tom King on suspicion of having stolen a horse, for which a reward was being offered. King cried out for Turpin to shoot and Turpin did, but he hit not the landlord (a certain Bayes), but King, who died.

Probably a more reliable account of King's death is that he was caught by the authorities and burnt to death for his crimes at Sutton Park. Local legend, one of the many associated with the restless souls of executed highwaymen, says that his ghost still haunts the place of his execution. Turpin himself was arrested on a charge of horse stealing and hanged at York on 10 April 1739. He was 34 years old.

Early issues of Midland newspapers such as *Aris's Birmingham Gazette* and the *Coventry Mercury* carried frequent testimony to the dangers of the road. As one experienced traveller wrote:

> "It is customary to have ten or a dozen guineas in a separate pocket as a tribute to the first who come to demand them."

It appears that those who paid up when asked were usually treated civilly, and often given a "password for the day" as an immunity from further highwaymen. This might have been true for a limited stretch of road, but it is hard to believe that highway robbery in the mid 18th century was so well organised for a "password" to be issued to every highwayman or footpad likely to work a route on a particular day.

Aris's Birmingham Gazette tells us that, on 18th May 1743:

> "The Birmingham Stagecoach was robb'd about 2 miles from Banbury, and about one hour after the robbery was committed, the noted Sansbury and his accomplice, who have infested these Roads were taken, being drunk, and asleep among the standing corn."

The "noted Sansbury" was executed shortly afterwards.

A touch of perverse chivalry seems to have been possessed by a highwayman described in *Aris's* for the 1st October 1750. The incident involved a Mr Henry Hunt of Birmingham who:

> "was stopped on Sutton Coldfield, in the Chester Road, by 2 highwaymen, who robb'd him of his Watch and Money but on Mr. Hunt asking him to give him back some silver the highwayman returned him 6 shillings, and immediately rode across the Coldfield, and robb'd another gentleman in sight of him, and then rode quite off."

On 6th May 1751 the same paper reported the stopping of the *Shrewsbury Caravan* by a highwayman with above average manners for his profession:

> "between the Four Crosses, and the Welsh Harp...a single highwayman, who behaved very civilly to the passengers, told them he was a tradesman in distress, and hoped they would contribute to his assistance, on which each passenger gave him something, to the amount, on the whole,

of about Four Pounds, with which he was mighty well
satisfied : but returned some half-pence to one of them
saying he never took copper. He then told them there
were two other collectors on the road, but he would
see them out of danger, which he accordingly did."

There are not many accounts of highwaymen from Staffordshire,
but a newpaper report of January 1761 describes one incident:

"several inhabitants of Lichfield were stopped on Whitt-
ington Heath on their return from Tamworth Market by a
single highwayman on a bay horse with a bald face. From
one, Mr Gregory, a dyer he took ninepence and a silver
coat button, from Mr Harvey Hartwell 9 or 10 shillings
and from a poor pie woman half a crown. Broughton,
an old man who sells linen cloth escaped by galloping
though his horse was loaded. The rogue fired a pistol
but happily missed him."

Contemporary accounts in the *Coventry Mercury* suggest a lot of
activity around the city. On the 30th September 1776 the Liverpool *Diligence* was stopped by a highwayman at Pickford Brook,
Allesley. A man and a woman riding in the vehicle had to hand
over £8 in cash and a finger ring. The same highwaymen also
hailed a stagecoach near Allesley the same night. But the driver
and guard had been warned by an account of the earlier robbery
that day and sped on to Coventry. The highwaymen chased the
coach to within 20 yards of the Spon End toll gate, where the
coach stopped and the passengers got out.

On 22nd April 1772 a lone highwayman stopped the Birmingham
coach to London near Chapel House. He took some £12 from the
passengers, and although there were eleven of them on the coach,
got clean away. The road between Kenilworth and Birmingham was
once busy with highwaymen and footpads. Early in January 1777,
a traveller on horseback was stopped by two highwaymen between
Coventry and Kenilworth. He was about to hand over some £15,
when the approach of other riders caused the villains to gallop
away empty handed.

Another incident, is reported in the *Coventry Mercury* for the
22nd December 1760:

"On Monday last, in the afternoon, as John Huff,
shoemaker, at Mockutt was riding in Dingley Fields,
betwixt Market Harborough and Sutton, he overtook a

person who proved to be a highwayman, for he had no sooner got up to him than the villain with his left hand seized the horse's bridle and with the right presented a pistol and demanded his money: but the horse stepping over a rut threw the rogue on his back and his fall frightening the creature occasioned him to set off at a gallop. However the highwayman managed to discharge his pistol after Mr. Huff, the ball from which made a hole through his coat skirt went betwixt one of his legs and the horse's belly and broke his stirrup leather, but happily did no other damage. The villain had a cape over his face, had on a light coloured greatcoat and his under coat was of purple colour."

From the same paper a week later on the 29th December 1760 comes the following:

"On Wednesday morning last, about 5 o'clock the Warrington and Chester Stagecoaches were stopped on Meriden Heath by a single highwayman mounted on a brown or bay horse, who robbed the passengers in the Warrington Stage of about L4 (4 guineas) and those in Chester of near L2. The villain lay on Monday and Tuesday nights last at the Bull's Head Inn, Meriden, from which place he departed but a short time before he committed the above robberies having ordered the hosteler to call him up by 4 o'clock in the morning. He is a middle sized man, wears a light coloured greatcoat and...was seen on Saturday last near Coleshill."

Although decreasing in number, highwaymen were still operating in the late 1770s. The following report is from *Piercy's Coventry Gazette* of March 1778:

"Highway Robbery. Coventry, January 16,1778. Whereas, Mr. Thomas Bucknall, of this city, rider to Messrs Eburne and Harrold, was stopt on Friday last, on the turnpike road between Stoke Common and the Toll Gate, by a highwayman who robbed him of 27 guineas in gold, and 9 shillings and 6d in silver, and rode off towards Binley, Brinklow, and Lutterworth..."

In June 1766, William Pare and Thomas Pestell were arrested while asleep in bed at the Stonebridge Hotel Inn. They had been involved in robbing the *Machine* near Coventry. A watch stolen from one of the passengers was found in their possession with two loaded pistols. The two men were imprisoned by Alderman Hewitt. Two others, William Wayner and James Bromwich were arrested for the same robberies, which included hold ups in Sherwood Forest. The watch mentioned, made of gold, was to be taken to Birmingham for sale.

On 10th July 1766 Wayner and Bromwich left Coventry Jail in a guarded coach heading for their trial at Nottingham Assizes. They were convicted on the charge of stealing 33 shillings from John Harle in Sherwood Forest and sentenced to death on 30th July. Both men were 22 or 23 years old.

Occasionally, highwayman, coachman and guard worked together. In October 1779. the Worcester *Diligence* was stopped and robbed several times on successive evenings by two highwaymen. On 11th October a guard was placed on the coach which was later stopped near Chipping Norton. The guard apparently allowed the highwaymen to rob the passengers at will, and £3 was stolen. It was not until they had ridden 100 yards that the guard aimed and fired his pistol after them. Afterwards the driver was overheard complaining that such men as a rule gave him a share of what they took. From his blatant disappointment and the behaviour of the guard, there seems no doubt that the highwaymen had some arrangement with the coachman that they failed to keep. Two years earlier there had been a similar case involving the driver and guard of a coach on the Gloucester road.

Some Midlands highwaymen earned quite a reputation for their deeds and their names are well known. The enigmatic Jonathan Wild (1682-1725) of Wolverhampton was not only a highwayman. He was also an organiser of criminals and, conversely, a thief catcher in league with the City Marshal. He was eventually arrested through a piece of stolen lace found in possession of an accomplice and after further evidence was given against him, Wilde was sentenced to death. While lying in the condemned cell he took poison, but the dose was insufficient to kill him and he was executed in a half dazed state. He was buried in St Pancras Churchyard, but his body was later stolen and the empty coffin found in the street. It is said that the corpse was taken back to Wolverhampton in a hearse, but no one has ever been able to discover if this is true or not.

Farnborough, near Fenny Compton, was the birthplace of Tom Hatton, a famous Warwickshire highwayman. Apparently he was another of the "gentleman" who robbed only the rich and was generous to the poor. He supposedly had a wonderful horse, and it was said that he rode with an enchanted bridle and could never be caught while mounted. After a run of many years and hundreds of hair breadth escapes Hatton was captured at Warwick, but he escaped even the hangman by hanging himself with the mat in his cell.

A few days before his suicide, Hatton told a visiting friend that he had hidden an iron box containing a silver cup filled with golden guineas in a field at Fenny Compton, known as the "Hen and Chickens". No search of the area has revealed anything.

Another well known Warwickshire highwayman was Bendigo Mitchell. He used the Old Inn at Bishops Tachbrook (now a private house) as his headquarters, and operated around Harwood House, east of Morton Morrell. A cunningly planned refuge said to have been used by highwaymen is to be found in the underground stable at a farm in Meriden, still known today as "Highwayman's House".

One of the most notorious of all Midlands highwaymen was John Hawkins, alias Yellow Jack. In 1773 he was convicted of various offences in Coventry and Warwickshire and sentenced to death, but this was commuted to transportation for life. Hawkins came back however, and tried to join the army. He might have got away with it if he had not argued with the recruiting sergeant before he kissed the Bible. Just as Hawkins was about to be sworn in, Alderman Hewitt who was administering the oath, recognised Yellow Jack and remembered his crimes. In December 1782 he was taken from Coventry jail by stagecoach to the coast, where he was put on a ship to the American plantations where he would spend the rest of his life.

For some years at the end of the 18th century, a gang of robbers and highwaymen from Culworth in Northamptonshire, terrorised the whole of the South Midlands. Their leader John Smith was known mainly as a pugilist, but apparently had some brains as well. His gang included his two sons and about twelve others. They always worked to a plan and Smith seems to have had a very effective intelligence system. Lone travellers, carriers and toll houses were easy prey.

A certain Mr Wright, a lawyer from Rugby going home from visiting a client at Field Burcot, was robbed of all his money and papers. Carriers returning from villages around Warwick and Stratford upon Avon were attacked, and toll houses on the

Southam to Banbury road were robbed of their takings. The gang were very active at the time of the great autumn fairs, Stratford producing the most victims, who were robbed of anything from a few pounds up to hundreds.

Eventually they were given away by the drunken carelessness of two of their number. John Smith and three other members were hanged at Northampton in August 1787, others were sentenced to transportation, while Smith's two sons were acquitted. John Smith the younger reverted to the old ways and took to highway robbery. Exactly two years after his father's execution he was arrested for a hold up at Gaydon (south of Leamington Spa) and hanged at Warwick. A young woman named Elizabeth Beere had been deeply attached to Smith. She recovered his body and, leaving Warwick at nightfall, brought it on a donkey for burial at Culworth.

Despite the predominance of highwaymen in literature, folklore and the public imagination, many highway robberies were the work of commonplace footpads. These were usually thugs who preyed mainly on the poorer classes of traveller, risking the gallows for scant rewards.

On 24 June 1774 both the Chester coaches were stopped by two footpads. One on the London - Shrewsbury road near Dunchurch (south of Rugby) the other a few miles west of Coventry. Both coaches held four passengers, and the footpads collected little, but did get away with one gentleman's brace of pistols

A coach was robbed on the Warwick road at Knowle by footpads who lay in wait behind some bushes. A gate provided easy access and, presumably, escape as well. During the robbery the coachman was killed, which gave rise to a story that his ghost could some- times be seen walking the fields on moonlit nights. A scare of this kind happened in 1918/19 when the "ghost" was seen by several people and many were afraid to go to the village. It turned out to be a butcher's errand boy.

Foot travellers always made much easier targets than coaches. On 22nd October 1767 "between the 115th and 116th milestone below Swynfen" (just south of Lichfield) a traveller was robbed by a foot- pad "armed with a horse pistol". A month later on 20th November, Matthew Butler and Francis Hamp were stopped and robbed at Frad- ley Common (near Lichfield) by two footpads, and one of them shot Hamp through the throat.

Few attacked by footpads were quite as unfortunate as Richard Armstrong, landlord of the Salutation Inn, Coventry in the 1780s. One night, while returning to Coventry over Stivichall Common, two men set a large dog onto his horse and beat him as he hung head downward in a ditch with one foot in a stirrup. The poor man was left in this painful predicament for almost two hours until a passing servant heard his cries for help.

The penalties for these crimes were severe, to suit the age. Highwaymen and footpads caught were usually hanged and mail robbers had always been. But this severity was evidently not a deterrent. It was not until the Earl of Leicester, Postmaster General in 1753, persuaded the government to have the bodies hung in chains by the roadside, that any significant decrease in robberies took place. This barbarous practice of gibbeting was not abolished until 1834.

There were many gibbets in the Midlands. Gibbet Hill, where Oscott College now stands, gained its name from the last few minutes in the life of a man who had robbed a London mercer on the Chester road. He had a cart pulled from under him in 1729. Around 1850 a number of skeletons thought to be the remains of executed criminals were unearthed from a stone pit at the south end of Burton Dassett ridge in south Warwickshire. The elevation on which they were found, known as "Gallows" or "Gibbet Hill", is not far from a crossroads. There were gibbets on Little Sutton Common and Washwood Heath near Birmingham. Names such as Gallows Green near Alton Towers, Gallows Brooke at Middleton north-east of Sutton Coldfield, and Gallows Hill just outside Warwick tell their story.

In many people's minds highwaymen and fast stagecoaches make a romantic mixture, but by the late 18th century the coaches usually went too fast and were too well guarded to be attacked. Roads were also improving and were now busier and faster than they had been since Roman times, so a lone highwayman was at a significant disadvantage.

There are very few records of highwaymen operating into the 19th century. Those hanged at Fisherton Jail, Salisbury between 1806 and 1824 are among rare examples. On the whole, the era of the highwayman was coming to an end by the early 1780s, and the arrival of the Royal Mail coaches in 1784, with their armed guards and locked strong boxes, practically finished them off. There is no record of a Royal mail coach being robbed by a highwayman.

Royal Mail

The Post Office derives its name from travellers hiring horses at stages, or posts, along their journey. They were said to be "riding post". The Royal Post was instituted in 1511 during the reign of Henry VIII (1509 - 1547), when the office "Master of the Posts" was established. He had to arrange relays of horses for despatch riders travelling on affairs of state. The four post roads then organised were London to Dover for cross channel communications, London to Plymouth for the King's dockyard, London to Scotland, and London to Chester for Ireland. In 1635 Thomas Witherings was appointed Master of the Posts and re-organised the system to provide an official means of sending letters around the country.

By 1632 postmasters had been settled in all the important towns of England, and in 1657 "The Post Office of England" was established by Act of Parliament.

It is recorded that in 1663 John Lax was the postmaster of Coventry, and amongst the state papers of the day is a letter to him by one Thomas Ibsen. Ibsen states his intention of settling horses between London and Chester for travellers to hire out at 3d per mile, but the various postmasters in the district voiced strong objections, as this was likely to take away their own profits.

In 1719 against opposition, Ralph Allen, a Cornishman living in Bath, introduced a service of postboys riding with the mail, at a speed of "not less than five miles per hour". The postboy (who could be any age from 16 to 60) is illustrated by a woodcut in an early edition of *Jobson's Coventry Mercury*. He is mounted on a well bred horse, dressed in jack boots, breeches, cut away coat and jockey hat, and blowing his posthorn to warn of his approach. The mail bags are behind him on the horse.

Postboys reached practically everywhere, and the complex system of bye and cross posts established and maintained by Allen was a great achievement. However, there were serious problems. The stipulated speed of 5 miles per hour was not usually achieved, the Post Office was suffering losses of around £80,000 a year through unauthorised conveyance of letters by stagecoaches and carriers, and postboys were frequent robbed by highwaymen and footpads. Even so, as late as the 1780s the Post Office was carrying mail by postboys on horseback, or occasionally by wheeled vehicles called "mail carts".

Reform was to come from outside the Post Office in the form of John Palmer, born in Bath in 1742, son of a brewer. Palmer was the successful manager of both the Bath and Bristol theatres whose business often suffered because of a poor postal service. His own private coach was almost twice as fast as the postboys, and it was much safer to deliver scripts and contracts himself rather than trust the mail service. When not able to travel himself he used a stagecoach which ran between Bristol, Bath and London in 17 hours, less than half the time taken by the postboys. Although it was illegal, stagecoaches often carried urgent letters disguised as parcels, which were not.

Palmer suggested to the Postmaster General that the mail should be carried by stagecoach, and that the coach should be built like his own; light, compact and committed to speed rather than comfort or roominess. The coach would have an armed guard, carry no more than four passengers and be exempt from paying tolls. Palmer's idea was presented to the General Post Office in the form of a report entitled *A Plan for the Reform and Improvement of the General Post Office*. It was not highly thought of until a presentation to William Pitt, who was then Chancellor of the Exchequer and with whom Palmer had some influence.

One result of the report was introduction of the "Mail Coach" in 1784, when the Post Office issued the following notice:

"His Majesty's post masters general, being inclined to make an experiment for the more expeditious conveyance of mails of letters by stage coaches, machines etc......... have been pleased to order that a trial should be made upon the road between London and Bristol to commence at each place on Monday 2nd August next."

The first Mail Coach performed the journey in one hour less than the stagecoach time for the route, and a new era was underway.

To ensure that the needs of the mail were met the Post Office laid down the departure times and operating timetable, paid an agreed fee per mile to contractors and provided the guard to enforce security and timekeeping. Passengers on the Royal Mail coaches took second place to the mail. If they were not ready after a stop they were simply left behind. In the interests of regular operation an

Taking up the Mails.

Hugh Thomson's sketches are concentrated in these central chapters because he was illustrating a ser-ialised feature about coaching in its prime. They add some life and movement that are not to be found in photos of milestones and the like.

approved standard of vehicle was decreed, though it did not come in immediately.

Palmer directed that all postmasters/postmistresses along the route must have their post bags sealed and ready to be picked up. At rural post offices where the coach did not change horses, mail for collection was put into a bag and held up on a cleft stick for the guard to grab. If there was mail to be delivered he tossed it down. Palmer also stated that toll gate keepers must open their gates when they heard the horn and the coach was not less than 250 yards away. If they failed they were fined 40 shillings. A Royal Mail coach was to stop for nothing unless the guard or horses were injured.

Palmer found it necessary to put up postal charges and close the night mail at London at 7 or 8 o'clock instead of midnight to get it away earlier.

Unlike ordinary stagecoaches at the time, whose stages ranged from 10 to 15 miles or more, the horses on the mails were changed every 6 to 8 miles. They were horsed by contractors who also provided the coachman, and for a short time, the guard. These were usually inn-keepers along the route who were were paid 3d per mile, the same rate as the postboys, which was later reduced to 1d a mile. Revenue from passengers and parcels (there was no parcel service outside of London until the 1880s) provided contractors with their profit. The innkeepers/contractors sometimes issued their own tokens for use at inns along the route. One such was a special token issued in honour of John Palmer and his mail coaches, called a "Mailcoach Halfpenny".

The mail coach was under the complete control of the guard, who was provided by the Post Office as their representative on board. He carried a brace of pistols, a cutlass and a blunderbuss, and would usually be someone accustomed to using firearms, such as an ex-soldier. The guards were immaculately turned out in scarlet coats and tall hats with a gold band around them. They had a list of twenty six instructions for carrying out their duties, and wages were around 10s.6d a week. This was not much, but generous tips and the privilege of the position made it attractive. On the "patent" mail coaches introduced as an improvement, the guard's "dickey seat" was raised at the rear of the coach, his feet resting on the mail box, but on early mail coaches he sat in front by the coachman.

A standard item of equipment for the guard was his three foot long coach horn, sometimes called the "yard of tin". On this he sounded calls such as "slacken pace", "clear the road" or "change horses". Some guards carried a keyed bugle, a more versatile instrument, though banned by the Post Office who felt it was too frivolous. During journeys the guard had to complete a timebill, entering times of arrival at stops as recorded by a locked time-piece sealed in a wooden case. He added explanations for any delays and returned the timebill to the Superintendent.

Each mail guard was in charge of the running of his coach, and the safety of both the coach and the mails it was carrying. When a coach was halted by snow drifts, floods, breakdown or anything else, the guard's first priority was to get the mail bags forward by taking one or both of the leading horses, going on foot if snow drifts proved impassable for them and hiring a post chaise as soon as he reached a town. He carried a tool kit in case of breakdown and was expected to make running repairs to the coach.

When a coachman named Garland pulled up the Bristol to Birmingham Mail in 1822, it was the guard, Pope, who sprung into action. He "instantly commenced severing with his axe the huge limbs of the tree" and supervised removal of the barrier when help arrived.

The extremely hard winter of 1836/7 put mail guards to the test. There was an exceptionally heavy snowfall with extensive drifting on Christmas night, and by 27th December fourteen mail coaches up and down the country were abandoned.

The mail coach guard's job was demanding and responsible. They did misbehave occasionally but there were fewer complaints about them than guards on the ordinary stagecoaches. The *Gloucester Journal* of 11 November 1811 carried this item:

> "the guard of the Gloucester and Hereford Mail Coach has been dismissed the service, by order of the inspector of Mail Coaches, and the Coachman by the Proprietor of the Coach, for behaving in a very abusive manner to a lady and another female passenger, the week before last, on the road from Gloucester to Ledbury."

The main problem with mail coach guards though, seems to have been an inclination to discharge their blunderbusses at farm animals and stray dogs, much to the alarm of passengers. During the wars with France in the early 1800s, guards were often awarded £5 by the Post Office for each escaped prisoner of war killed or wounded. Apparently it was not thought worth the trouble to try and recapture them. This gave guards another excuse for indiscriminate firing and the situation became so serious that an Act of Parliament of 1811 forbade firing except in defence, on pain of a fine of £5.

The guards proved ample protection against highwaymen and footpads, and there is no record of a robbery of a Royal Mail coach by either class of criminal. When the mails were occasionally robbed it was in more clandestine ways. On 4th April 1803 the Chester Mail coach going through Barnet to London, with mails from Lutterworth, Hinckley, Atherstone, Tamworth, Burton on Trent, Market Drayton and Nantwich, was robbed. The mail was packed in a leather sack and included were many bills, that is, Bills of Exchange, which were not unlike cheques and which in those days could easily be appropriated. Somehow this was stolen from the coach on its way to London and the empty sack found in a pond weighed down with bricks.

In April 1801 new postal rates were implemented, starting at 3d (1.25p) for letters to be sent no more than 15 miles from any post office, and increasing in proportion the the distance. In the same year from the Birmingham Post Office it was possible to send letters to America, to where the mails departed on the first Wednesday in every month, to Lisbon once a fortnight, and to the West Indies on every Wednesday in the month, among many other places. However, when the cost of postage is related to the average weekly wage of 10 to 15 shillings, it becomes apparent that only the relatively well off could afford the service.

By the late 1780s about twenty mail coach services radiated from London, including routes to Birmingham, Shrewsbury and Worcester. In 1808 the Post Office extended the Oxford, Birmingham and Shrewsbury mail route to join the Holyhead Road at Bangor via central Wales. This supplemented the old route via Chester, which continued. There were also fourteen or more cross posts between provincial centres. According to Post Office schedules, Bristol was reached from London in 15 hours, Holyhead in 44 hours 50 minutes, and Edinburgh in 57 hours 50 minutes. Actual journey times would have been a few minutes longer as the time in each district still depended on its longitude, Greenwich Mean Time not then existing.

To be on a mail coach route was particularly important to a provincial town. It contributed to its economy, boosted its sense of importance and brought the earliest news of important events.

Royal Mail Coach built about 1820, now in Science Museum, London

Photo: Science & Society Picture Library

(56)

At moments of national excitement thousands gathered to await the mails. News of Wellington's victory over Napoleon at Waterloo came to Lichfield on 20th June 1815 by the London mailcoach. It was decked out with Union Jacks fluttering in the wind, the guard sounded his horn, and the outside passengers shouted the news to people in the streets.

The mail coach did not achieve its characteristic appearance as soon as Palmer's new system was implemented. The first Royal Mail coach was little more than an ordinary, light, post coach mounted fairly high on elbow springs, with a locked boot over the rear axel and a guard sitting by the driver. Such vehicles proved too fragile for the arduous new work, and coaches to a design patented by coach builder John Besant were adopted in December 1787. Use of such patent coaches was a condition of the contract between the Post Office and the contractors.

Soon after the adoption of the patent mail coach, Besant entered into partnership with another coach builder, John Vidler, but then died suddenly. It was Vidler, then, who built, owned and maintained the mail coaches from his works at Millbank, London, until the contract expired in 1836. Although Vidler actually sold a few of his coaches at a set price of £140 each, he usually hired them out on a mileage basis, and was responsible for servicing and repairs. At first, through lack of organisation, coaches were often sent out without being greased or cleaned, but this soon changed. In 1792 Vidler had one hundred and twenty coaches for which he charged 2.5d per double mile, including maintenance and repair.

In addition to various innovations which proved unworkable, the patent mail coach introduced two of lasting importance. The rear boot with guard's seat on top was built as part of the main coach body, and the wheels were more securely fastened by what became known as the "mail axle". Despite these innovations the body was still suspended from the coachman's box at the front by leather straps and passengers suffered from the ceaseless, sickening sideways sway.

According to the Birmingham inventor and manufacturer Matthew Boulton, writing in 1798, the Besant coach was so uncomfortable that after a journey in one to Exeter, he was far from surprised to learn from the landlady of the inn that:

"passengers who arrived every night were obliged to go supperless to bed; and unless they go back to the old-fashioned coaches, long and a little lower, the mail-coaches will lose all their custom."

In 1804 a major design change resulted from the combination of the coachman's box with the main body and rear boot. This single unit could be mounted on horizontal springs, thus reducing the height of the vehicle to improve stability. This feature was adopted generally in the early 1800s, and though the mail coach was important in publicising it, no one knows for certain who was the inventor.

In its later form, the box seat with angled footboard was in two sections divided by side irons. The driver's part was unpadded in case he should feel too comfortable and doze off, but the forward passenger seat was well upholstered. Because mail coaches travelled mainly at night, good lighting was essential. A three aspect lamp was fitted to the centre front of the footboard, and there were two headlamps and two smaller sidelamps on either side of the front body above wheel level.

The livery of the Royal Mails was at first blue and orange, but soon black and maroon became standard. The fore boot carried the Royal Cipher "GR" in gold, and the window, lower part of the door, side panels, wheels, axles and undercarriage were generally maroon. The base of the box boot and upper panels of the body were black. The Royal Arms were painted on the door panel, and the four upper quarters carried the stars of the senior orders of chivalry. The number of the coach was painted on the hind boot.

Although relatively few in number, the mail coaches did have some initial impact on the coaching industry. In the early 1780s stagecoaching concentrated on short and medium distance routes radiating from London. Outside a 120 mile radius of the capital the network was sparse and services sporadic.

Stagecoaches at this time managed an average speed of between 6 and 6.4 miles an hour (including stops). Palmer confidently predicted 8 or 9 miles per hour for his mail coaches. On the Bristol road such speeds were attained at an early date, but this was an exception. The scheduled average for nineteen mail coach services from London in 1792 was only 7.25 miles per hour including stops. In 1797 for twenty routes from the capital it was 7.08 miles per hour. Slower still were provincial cross country and branch routes, averaging only 6.32 mph.

Even so, these figures show improvement on contemporary stage-coach services, and Mail coaches also had a better reputation for time keeping and reliability. With the exclusiveness of having fewer outside passengers and the safety provided by the armed guard, they attracted a select clientele.

The situation did not remain like this very long. The horses and coachman for a mail coach were provided by the proprietor, and most major London and provincial proprietors operated both mail and stagecoaches. The innovatory elements of Palmer's mail coach system could be swiftly evaluated and adopted for stagecoaches. Proprietors soon developed and improved their own services using coaches of the same general pattern, so that often the only difference between the stage and the mail coaches would be their livery. Their loads varied more, stagecoaches sometimes carrying as many as fourteen people on the roof, as well as those inside.

Regular mail coaches between London and Birmingham began as early as 1785. There is a directory entry for 1801 describing a London Mail Coach setting out "every afternoon at Three o'clock" from the Dog Inn, Spiceal Street, Birmingham. Two years later in May 1803, the following advert appeared in *Aris's Birmingham Gazette:*

SWAN HOTEL BIRMINGHAM

THE Public are most respectfully informed, the BIRMINGHAM, COVENTRY, and LONDON ROYAL MAIL sets out from the above INN every Afternoon at Three o'clock.
Inside Fare 2gns 2s. - Outside Fare 1gn 1s.
Performed by Barton and Co.

[Presumably £2.4s and £1.2s]

In the same advert a "Post Coach" travelling to London from the same inn (and put on by the same proprietor) via Coventry, Daventry, Stoney Stratford and Dunstable, charged half the mail coach fares.

On the 26th May 1812 great celebrations were reported in Birmingham because of a new mail coach to London. It was "attended by 8 mail guards, in full uniform and adorned with blue ribbons", and the entourage "paraded the streets for 2 hours". After this the coachman and guards were

"feasted with wine, biscuits and sandwiches, and the Mail
set out for London from the Swan Hotel, amid the ringing
of the St. Martin's bells and the cheering of the assembled thousands."

Obviously drinking and driving was not a serious offence.

The other four mails leaving the Swan Hotel in 1812 were the daily
services to Sheffield, Manchester, Coventry, and Nottingham/Derby.
In the same year, the Hen & Chickens Hotel, New Street, were
running mails to Bristol, Manchester, Sheffield and Nottingham.

In April 1825 the Swan Hotel was advertised as a "New Royal Mail
Establishment" run by J Hart. He announced the departure of a

"New Royal Mail Coach", leaving every morning at 8 o'
clock and going through "Coventry, Nuneaton, Hinckley,
Leicester, Melton and Oakam to STAMFORD, from
whence it will return every day".

Early in 1830 *Aris's* displayed the following advert:

ALTERATION OF ROYAL MAILS

THE Public is respectfully informed, that by arrangements
made with his Majesty's Post Master General, the LONDON
MAIL will arrive at the *Swan Hotel* Coach-office at *half
past seven in the morning;* and the DUBLIN, HOLYHEAD,
SHREWSBURY, DUDLEY, STOURBRIDGE, KIDDER-
MINSTER, BEWDLEY, and STOURPORT ROYAL MAILS
will *depart* from the above Office at a *quarter before eight*
every morning, being half an hour *earlier* than heretofore.

THE ROYAL MAIL to LONDON will start from the
Swan Office as usual, every evening at a quarter before six
o'clock, and by the new arrangement, is driven through by
two coachmen only, viz. one from Birminham to Stoney
Stratford, and one from thence to London.

THOMAS WADDELL and Co. Proprietors.

In 1835 Thomas Waddell announced in *Aris's* a

"NEW AND IMPORTANT COMMUNICATION THROUGH LINCOLNSHIRE AND NORFOLK, BY A NEW ROYAL MAIL FROM BIRMINGHAM".

This was to run from the Swan every morning at a quarter to eight, ultimately arriving at Yarmouth early next morning, "being timed throughout at the rate of nine miles per hour".

In that year (1835) during the heyday of coaching, the Hen & Chickens alone ran eight mail coaches daily. In smaller Midland towns such as Ludlow the number was considerably fewer, three mails leaving daily in 1834. Evesham was similar, with two daily Mail departures in 1835, whilst Malvern seems to have had none. More important coaching centres in the Midlands were Worcester and Shrewsbury, both with five mails daily in 1834.

In the late 18th century the London to Birmingham Mail had taken 36 hours but by the mid 1830s this had been cut to 11 hours. The *New London Royal Mail* started running from the capital on New Year's Day 1836. It was one of a fleet of fast mails which were apparently so punctual that villagers on their routes could set the clocks by them. In the same year the Holyhead Mail was thought to be performing miracles when it covered the 260 miles from London in 26 hours and 55 minutes. This was the fastest time it ever achieved and a huge improvement on the 38 hours in 1817.

There is no doubt that the mail coach brought new glamour and excitment to the road, The English Romantic writer Thomas De Quincey (1785-1859) described an incident in his essay *The English Mail Coach*:

> "Once I remember being on the box of the Holyhead Mail, between Shrewsbury and Oswestry, when a tawdry thing from Birmingham, some *Tally Ho* or *Highflier,* all flaunting with green and gold came up alongside of us. What a contrast to our royal simplicity of form and colour is this plebian wretch! ... the beast ... had as much writing on its sprawling flanks as would have puzzled a decipherer from the tombs of Luxor."

For a while the coaches ran side by side, but after a while the Birmingham coach tried to pass. De Quincey was most upset; the audacity of such a vehicle daring to challenge the supremacy of the mail, let alone overtake it. He need not have worried, the mail coach driver spurred on his superior horses leaving the Birmingham coach far behind in its dust.

Racing the Mail

Throughout its existence the Post Office had been troubled by the carrying of mails other than by mail coaches. This "illegal conveyance of letters" was "carried on to a very great extent", according to the Solicitor to the Post Office in the early 19th century. In Birmingham at this time, "the practice [did] exist to a very considerable extent", and by 1830 the amount of letters sent via stagecoaches around the country were, "in all probability equal to one half those conveyed through the post office."

It was no secret that country carriers had acted as an unofficial postal service since the late 17th century, and by the early 19th century illegal conveyance was still most common at the local level. In Birmingham it was well known that carriers were employed by local merchants and factories

"to take out notes or orders for goods to the small manufacturers residing in neighbouring villages". [The carriers did not try to conceal this traffic and often put signs over their doors] "stating that they convey from Walsall to Birmingham or to any other place and such and such times". [A man from Walsall knew] "instances of more than 120 letters being sent in the course of a day by one particular house", [and that the average through the year would] "exceed 50 letters daily".

There were twenty or thirty houses to which the carriers regularly called, each of them sending perhaps eight or nine letters a day.

People giving information to the Post Office which lead to a conviction for the offence would usually be rewarded with 50 shillings or more.

Mail coaches are familiar, and it is not often realised they were few and that they were never dominant in the coaching industry. By 1804 there were still only 137 patent mail coaches in England and Wales, though by 1834 they had increased to 261. Numbers rose no higher. At the same time there were around 3000 stage-coaches, so mail coaches accounted for only 8% of all coaches used for public transport.

By the early 1820s stagecoach competition caused the Post Office to demand higher speeds from its coaches. By 1836 the mail coaches on sixteen main routes were running at an average speed of 9.21 miles per hour overall, including stops. The London to Bristol via Marlborough service was one of the fastest, averaging 10.3 mph, but some stagecoaches could match this. For the mails the Post Office's demands caused their own problems, and in February 1835 alone, nine mail coaches overturned.

Fares on a mail coach were usually higher than on ordinary stage-coaches. They also varied widely from route to route, depending on the degree of competition. A survey by the Post Office in 1837 covering all main routes out of London, showed that the average mail fare was 4.9d (2p) per mile for inside passengers, and 2.6d per mile for outside. The corresponding figures for night stage-coaches were 4.3d and 2.2d. But competition was based not on fares so much as speed and quality of service. As the passenger traffic increased, improved roads and coach building techniques allowed higher speeds and heavier loads, so the day stagecoaches were able to compete realistically in speed, comfort and safety.

A further problem for the mail coach system was that, despite increased payments from the Post Office, most mail contractors ran at a loss. Higher speeds increased costs while the lucrative passenger traffic diminished. Travellers increasingly found mail fares too expensive and their night schedules too inconvenient, and instead travelled by the growing number of fast day coaches.

It seems that the mail contractors were prepared to work at such a loss because the prestige of the mails, with their reputation for speed and punctuality, had a positive effect on their other coaches and inns. W Horne stated that "We have often horsed a coach for nothing at all, because it leads to other advantages."

A "Royal Mail Coach Office" (such as The Swan in Birmingham), suggested that the best coaches ran from there and attracted more custom. But this was not enough, the Post Office was still obliged to keep up their high speeds and profits remained meagre. Birmingham proprietor John Hart told a House of Lords Committee in 1832 "I worked 3 of His Majesty's Mails that did not pay me". Things were not to improve. One of the main proprietors of the mail coaches, William Chaplin, echoed popular feeling when in 1835 he declared that "mails unfortunately do not flourish except in very populous towns".

Whilst the stagecoach network continued to expand during the early to mid 1830s, that of the mail coaches remained static. Services on the main post roads from London formed a network of 4,554 miles in 1810, which had fallen to 4,424 miles by 1835. Between these dates only one major new mail coach service was introduced, a direct route to Edinburgh avoiding York, but it attracted few passengers and was not a success. Some services had even been discontinued, such as London to Holyhead via Chester, in 1828.

"Driving to catch the mail"

Misadventure

British coach travel in the early 19th century was a great improvement on what had gone before, but still hazardous. It probably had a higher rate of death and injury per passenger mile than any other form of public transport, before or since. However, the number of people travelling by coach was relatively small, and in any accident it was unusual for more than one or two to be killed. This was bad enough, but does not compare to a crowded train crashing at higher speed.

The accident rate for stage and mail coaches was high in part because they rode too high off the ground. This made them liable to overturn, especially when overloaded with passengers as they often were, and it was not unknown for people to topple over the side. Other major causes of accidents included horses bolting, parts of the coach breaking or coming loose, severe weather, horses overrunning on a hill due to the ineffective skid pan brake (when used), and reckless or negligent driving by the coachman.

Accidents involving deaths or severe injuries always made good material for newspapers, which often gave them whole columns. Accidents which might not appear were minor occurrences in out of the way places, or involved people not deemed newsworthy. This was obviously not the case when the *Shrewsbury Wonder* was involved in an accident in 1840. A newspaper report lists the passengers as M Theophile Van de Woestyne, attache to the Belgian Embassy, his brother and their valet, Count Pollem, the Sardinian Minister and his valet, a consulting surgeon from Gloucester and three other gentlemen.

The editor of *Leisure Hour* declared that he could "fill a whole sheet" with details of the calamities he had experienced while travelling by coach:

> "We have gone bodily, with a dozen companions, over a hedge into a bean field; we have burst through the crust of a gravel pit.......... and been deposited in the ditch; we have come down with a crash on the stones through collision with a waggon, when a fellow passenger was killed on the spot; we have been left in the snow on a moonless night in consequence of the driver nodding

on his box; and we have come to grief in various ways,
as well as through weather or unavoidable accident, as
by the neglect, the thoughtlessness, and the insobriety
of those to whom the public safety was confided."

Although the Post Office usually went to great lengths to
ensure that its coaches were regularly serviced and checked
for defective parts, this was not always the case with stagecoach proprietors, especially in the early 19th century. Many
accidents were caused by weak or damaged parts of the coach
or harness. Even parts that seemed in good order could give
way at any moment and without notice.

The front axle of the Worcestershire *Telegraph* once broke
at the bottom of Hanwell Hill, causing the coach to crash
onto its side. This caused serious injury to the coachman and
passengers, which included two ladies of whom "little hope
was entertained of recovery".

A less obvious and well known cause of injury and accident
were stones flung up by the hooves of the leading horses. This
is how Mr Webb, innkeeper of the George and Lichfield's
largest coach proprietor, lost two of his best horses on 14th
June 1817. They were killed at almost the same moment and
cost him 100 guineas (£105).

A coaching accident was a miserable scene. The Birmingham
"poet" John Freeth (c1730-1808), described a spill on the road
in the late 18th century:

> "Here a wheel lost a spoke,
> There an axletree broke,
> At the third place the perch snapped in two,
> A girl lost an eye,
> A man smashed his thigh,
> And the rest were beat black and blue,
> Then the horses one night,
> From hard driving took fright,
> And rushed down the hill helter-skelter,
> Whilst the passengers all,
> Both great and small,
> Were left in duck's puddle to welter."

On 30th September 1820 there was an appalling accident to
the *Aurora* day coach from London, which was crowded in
and out with passengers travelling to the Worcester Music

Festival. In descending Severn Stoke Hill the coachman failed to attach the skid brake to the wheel, and the speed gathered overturned the coach soon after rounding the bend at the bottom. Mr Bennet, organist of Christ College, Oxford was killed instantly, and a Mr Hughes, a glover from Sidbury, Worcester died next morning. Several other passengers were seriously injured. The inquest jury refused to return a verdict of manslaughter against the coachman.

On 5th October 1820 the Worcester and London *Fly* returning from Worcester was upset at Stoughton Bridge and all fourteen passengers were hurt. A lady had an arm broken, a "poor woman" her arm broken with various contusions, and a gentleman his hip dislocated. No explanation was given. In the next week the *Aurora* and *Royal Sovereign* Worcester to London day coaches were both upset and a number of the passengers injured.

Royal Mail coaches were not immune from accidents. A report in the *Coventry Mercury* for 7th November 1785:

> "A few nights since, the Birmingham Mail Coach twice overturned: the first time on Whitley Common near this city, the second time on Branston Bridge. What the effect of the former was we cannot say, but as to the latter, the guard was dashed against the battlements of the bridge, as were the two passengers, who, we are informed took post horses from Daventry to London. On Saturday the 29th the Holyhead Mail Coach was overturned near Stone in Staffordshire: it had only one passenger, one of HM Messengers who was so much hurt that he was obliged to stay at Stone. A few days since, the Liverpool coach was overturned by the breaking of the axle tree in the town of Wolverhampton. The inside passengers received only some slight bruises, but the coachman and two outside passengers were much hurt."

On the Holyhead Road just past Potterspury Lodge in Northamptonshire are the Gullet Hills, where Telford improved the road for a distance of 1,540 yards. At the top of the rise is Plumpark, formerly one of the several Royal hunting parks which were once such a feature of south Northamptonshire. Here was the scene of a "fearful coaching accident" in August 1837, when the horses of the *Emerald* coach from London to Birmingham ran away, overturning the coach and throwing outside passengers 20 feet. All were injured and one died.

Next along the Holyhead Road at the turn to Paulerspury is a memorial to the young victim of a rather different coaching accident. December 23rd 1840 was extremly cold and Richard Andrews, a 17 year old from Shrewsbury got down from the coach to run and warm himself. In doing so he slipped, fell under the moving coach and was killed instantly.

The Manchester to London *Red Rover* had a serious accident travelling through Staffordshire in 1836:

> "The horsekeeper declares...he had hold of the leaders, but, understanding that the coachman had mounted the box, he quitted his hold and the horses started off. The horrified outside passengers began to bale out and, as so often in this situation, sustained serious injury. Soon the horses were on the full gallop, and had a terrific appearance...On arriving at Tillington...near Stafford the coach was upset."

Horses on the Bristol to Birmingham *Hero* were fortunate in 1821. Stopped on Tewkesbury Bridge while the coachman strolled across to talk to his "opposite", they suddenly turned round and headed back the way they had come. Some people attempted to stop them, but this panicked the leaders who leapt over the side of the bridge. Luckily the horses were suspended in harness, where they remained until they could be hauled back again.

Occasionally coaching accidents had more malevolent causes, as noted by the *Coventry Mercury* for 9th September 1782:

> "Early yesterday morning the Liverpool post coach going between Coleshill and Lichfield was overthrown by some evil minded person or persons laying some timber across the road by which accident the coachman (Samuel Ford) was killed on the spot and a young woman an outside passenger had a leg and arm broke: happily the company within, three persons received no material injury."

Not all accidents occurred while the coach was in motion. The Birmingham to London *Eclipse* began in 1824 and was a famous coach in its day. The driver Ned Hassall and guard, Tom Peck, were well known on the road. They had been together on the coach for many years and were close friends. Ned was a Birmingham man, while Tom Peck came from Coventry.

One very frosty day in Coventry, the horses of the *Eclipse* were being changed as usual at the Craven Arms. As Peck was lifting up luggage behind the coach, the luggage strap broke, his foot slipped and he fell backwards onto the pavement. His head struck the kerb and he died instantly. At seeing his friend fatally injured Ned Hassall immediately fainted, and the shock was so great that he remained a helpless lunatic for the rest of his life.

A slightly similar incident, curiously enough involving the same coach, concerned the callous inhumanity of a certain Robert Eson, employed as a porter by Waterhouse at the Angel Inn, Islington. One day in August 1828 Elizabeth Semirot, a young Frenchwoman, was climbing up when the horses jerked suddenly forward, she fell and was fatally injured. A passing grocer, John West, said that the porter made no effort to catch or help the woman, but tried to prevent others from helping and was very abusive. Thomas Crowder, another observer, claimed that when he and others expressed sorrow at the incident, Eson used obnoxious language to them.

Drunken driving has a long history. A horrific report in the *Coventry Herald* on 9th April 1830 described how Peter Smith, a watchmaker, saw the London to Liverpool *Standard* overturn in Coventry with ten passengers aboard. It was half past midnight:

> "When it turned the corner, there seemed a great confusion amongst the horses... ; the fire that struck from the horses' feet was like a flash of lightening and instantly the coach fell over."

Smith saw the guard staggering up behind the coach - "the side of his face was all over blood". An outside passenger was heard muttering "Bad management! Bad management!" Another watchmaker, John Gutteridge, also hurried to the scene and helped the coachman, Thomas Platt, to his feet.

> "I think he was in a state of intoxication, he smelled very strong of liquor, and was very unsteady...; he was sick ... I saw him heaving... He said he was hurt and groaned."

Gutteridge now turned his attention to another victim of the accident, William Cooper, who was now visible by the light of a candle brought by Reverend Grindon. Cooper was lying in the road with a heavy white box on his head, covered in blood which was gushing from his ear. The watchmaker removed the box - "I picked him up in my arms and brought him to Mr. Grindon's house", where he died shortly afterwards.

The *Gloucester Journal* of 22nd December 1806 reported yet another incident:

"Melancholy Accident

On Monday evening last, as the Bristol and Birmingham mail-coach was coming down the hill between Alveston and Thornbury, in this county, the coachman, John Fishlock, being much intoxicated, and the night very dark, fell from the box, and one of the wheels passing over his neck, he was killed on the spot. The guard, William Giller, observing the accident, instantly got down, and endeavoured to stop the horses; but, finding themselves at liberty, they got into full speed, and he was unable to effect his purpose. With great activity and presence of mind, however, he regained his place behind, whence he got to the box, and drove the coach in safety to Thornbury. Giller immediately returned on horseback, in search of the unfortunate man, who he found totally lifeless; and the Coroner's Inquest have since returned a verdict, 'Accidental Death'. He has left a wife and two children.

On New Years Day 1830 the *Telegraph* coach which ran between Birmingham and Sheffield via Lichfield, failed to arrive at Lichfield. Later that day the waiting passengers learned that it was a total loss. Descending Swinscoe Hill, 3 miles from Ashbourne, Derbyshire the coachman was thrown from the box. The horses came down the hill at full speed, crossed the bridge at the bottom, and took the coach violently against the wall of a public house on the other side. One of the wheels was torn off but the coach hurtled on, hit the gate post of the toll bar and was smashed to pieces. Two inside passengers and the guard had jumped out, the one passenger who had stayed inside was severely injured.

The *Staffordshire Advertiser* noted the probable cause of the incident:

"The guard and coachman, it is feared, were far from sober, as they had called at many inns on the road to drink, in commemoration of the day."

It was known for passengers to sue for damages in such circumstances. In 1819 the proprietors of the *Umpire* which travelled from Liverpool to London via Lichfield, were sued

"Mr Pickwick had just drawn in his head, and Mr Wardle, exhausted with shouting, had done the same, when a tremendous jolt threw them forward against the front of the vehicle. There was a sudden bump - a loud crash - away rolled a wheel, and over went the chaise."

(*The Pickwick Papers*)

by passengers after an accident near Northampton. They had been thrown off the top of the coach by the drunken driver running up a bank and won £300.

Many coaching accidents were the result of coachmen from rival concerns racing for personal honour or the reputation of their employers. The narrowness of many roads meant there were regular minor accidents between vehicles trying to overtake. In their eagerness to outsmart their rivals, especially when trying to keep to schedule, proprietors were often prepared to put passengers at alarming risk. Coachmen sometimes had specific instructions not on any account to let a rival overtake them. This resulted in such racing that horrified passengers sometimes jumped off the coach rather that risk staying aboard.

The Holyhead Road was famous for its fierce competition. Though it seems rather doubtful, the *Tally-Ho!* and the *Independent Tally-Ho!* were quoted as running some stages at over 18 miles an hour. If true this was faster than the first cars were allowed to go at the start of the 20th century.

In the 1830s, the rival coaches *Nimrod* and *Wonder* were on the Shrewsbury run along the Holyhead Road and often raced each other. In 1835 the *Stag* was introduced by the owners of the *Wonder* - "to prevent the celebrated *Wonder* being in any way injured by racing." It is said that all three coaches might arrived at The Peacock, Islington together, and 2 hours ahead of time.

It is recorded that on May Day each year drivers and horses "were spurred to super-human and super-equine exertions" in attempts to beat all existing records. On 8th May 1830 the *Coventry Chronicle* published an item under the heading "Extra-ordinary Travelling":

> "Saturday being May Day, the usual competitions took place between the London coaches. The *Independent Tally Ho,* running between Birmingham and London, performed a feat altogether unparalleled in the annals of coaching, having travelled the distance of one hundred and nine miles in 7 hours and 39 minutes."

Many proprietors did not approve of such behaviour, as is shown by the following notice from *Aris's* in April 1831:

NELSON HOTEL
COACH RACING

It has been customary for the Day Coaches from London to Birmingham to exhibit their speed by Racing on the 1st of May - a practice attended with considerable danger.

CHARLES RADENHURST very respectfully informs his Friends, that he has given positive orders to his Coachmen to travel on that day at the regular speed, at which he considers as rapid a pace as they can travel with safety (viz ten miles per hour). Any of his coachmen disobeying the above orders, on representation to the Proprietors shall be immediately discharged.

Birmingham, April 23, 1831.

The drivers of Royal Mail coaches were not immune from recklessly trying to improve their times. In 1820 on the Holyhead Road a mile from St Albans, the Holyhead Mail tried to pass the Chester Mail by racing up on the wrong side of the road. The Chester coachman thoughtlessly pulled his leaders into his rival's path, the coaches were smashed into a heap and one passenger was killed. The inquest found both coachmen guilty of manslaughter, for which they were imprisoned.

The appearance of railways in the 1830s put great pressure on Royal Mail coaches. Greater and greater speeds were demanded to compete effectively leading to yet more accidents. One example comes from a GPO minute:

"Collision between the Holyhead Mail coach and the Manchester Mail coach, 29 June, 1838, at Dirty House Hill, between Weedon and Foster's Booth... [Northants] Both coachmen were at fault. The Holyhead coach had no lamps, and the explanation of their absence was that 28th June of that year was the Coronation Day of our beloved Queen, and the crowd was so great in Birmingham that, in paying attention to getting the horses through the streets, and having lost considerable time in doing so, in the hurry to get the coach off again the guard did not ascertain if the lamps were with the coach or not. The Manchester Coach, at the time of the accident, was attempting when climbing the hill, to pass the Carlisle mail coach, and was ascending on the wrong side of the

(73)

road. The horses dashed into each other, with the result
that one of the wheel horses of the Holyhead mail.....
was killed, and the others injured, one of the leaders
seriously. The harness was old, and snapped like chips,
or more serious would have been the consequences."

Severe weather in the form of frosts, thunderstorms or gales,
did not usually stop coach services. Sometimes though, a coach
might be whirled along by the wind in exposed areas. In 1822
a hurricane struck western Britain which caused much damage,
including blowing over the Holyhead to Shrewsbury mail twice
between Tyn y maes and Capel Curig in North Wales. Roads
were strewn with uprooted trees, causing further damage. On
turning a corner near Kempsey, in Worcestershire, the Birmingham to Bristol mail was faced by a tree of enormous size
"which, but for the adroitness of the coachman (Garland) in
pulling up his horses...might have proved fatal."

But it was exceptionally heavy snowfall and particularly
floods which were most dreaded, as a seasoned traveller of
the time noted:

"Give me a collision, a broken axle and an overturn, a
runaway team, a drunken coachman, snowstorms, howling
tempests; but Heaven preserve us from floods!"

In 1829 a bridge in Cheshire gave way during floods, casting
the Birmingham to Liverpool mail into the swollen River Wea-
ver. The coachman, named Bell, was thrown amongst the flailing
horses, but managed to reach the bank despite injury. The guard
Moreton was swept along until he grabbed hold of a tree, onto
which he clung for an hour before being thrown a rope and res-
cued "almost as much dead as alive". One "thin, active young
man" was able to squeeze through the coach window, "but
others too lusty to pass" perished inside. The coach was
swept away with the three horses which also drowned.

On 11th September 1829 the Birmingham and Liverpool mail
approached Smallwood Bridge not realising that the force of
the water had blown the bridge apart; the coach carried on
and was thrown into the river. At Powick Bridge near Worcester in 1802, the Malvern coach was swept downstream in a
flooded River Team, but luckily floated safely to the bank.

Heavy snows could also be disastrous to coach services. Mails
had a better accident record than the stagecoaches for much
of the coaching era, but they still had their problems, and

many were caused by snow. In the severe winter of 1798-9 snow fell thick and continuously through late January and early February. Many mail coaches missing on 1st February were not accounted for by the end of April.

The golden age of coaching in the 1820s and 30s saw many hard winters, and snowstorms over the Christmas period of 1836 were particularly severe. All roads in the Midlands were blocked, and seventeen coaches were stuck on Dunsmore Heath, south-east of Coventry. The Holyhead mail was amongst the casualties, and the guards had to unharness the horses and try to deliver the mails on horseback. Conditions were so bad in places that they still floundered.

The *Coventry Standard* on Friday 30th December 1836 reported that the harshness of the weather:

> "has been extraordinary in the last week. On Saturday, Sunday and Monday night the wind blew with great violence and the fall of snow (especially on the Sunday) has been tremendous. We believe such a rapid accumulation and such a sudden stoppage on the roads has not been known for these 20 years. The principle stoppage appears to have been on the road between Weedon and Dunchurch. Several hundred men have been employed to clear away the snow, and now have so far succeeded so that the mails carrying 2 days' papers and letters arrived in this city yesterday morning..."

The Sunday mentioned was Christmas Day. By that time the mail coaches to London had already been brought to a standstill at Dunchurch and the passengers accommodated at the Dun Cow and Green Man. The passengers were distressed at not being home for Christmas, but at least kept warm and dry, and in the evening a party was held at the Dun Cow. To complete their involuntary stay, coachmen and passengers organised a shoot for Boxing Day and a hare was bagged for the pot. Afterwards the party walked along the Rugby Road singing an assortment of carols, and were rewarded by local farmers with pork pies and elderberry wine.

Dense fogs did not altogether stop traffic but caused accidents. The Duke of Beaufort, a prime mover in the coaching revival of the early 1860s, had his own rule for driving on a foggy night. This involved pulling the coach up and putting out most of the lamps because there was a better view without them, the light being liable to shine in the coachman's eyes. However some kind of light was needed at night. What the coachman required was a thick piece of leather "covering rather more than half the flame" of the lamp. This would show the ditch or fence on each side and light up the road sufficiently, but would not come back off the fog into the driver's eyes.

Strange things could happen on the road. It was common for a wheel to come off or an axel to break, but a most unusual accident happened to the *Salopian* between Shifnal and Wolverhampton on a winter's day in 1845. The coach was going as its usual pace when the guard, who had gone forward to the box to talk to the driver, heard a loud crash behind. Turning he saw "to his amazement and dismay" the rear seat of the coach lying in the road some 30 yards behind and four passengers on the ground. One passenger was taken up dazed and senseless and the others were "more or less bruised".

The guard of a coach travelling from Dudley to Wednesbury was found to be missing from his place. He was found on the road having fallen off the "dickey seat" at the back of the coach, probably while dozing off.

One evening in January 1790 the *Balloon* coach from Birmingham arrived at the Bear Inn, Coventry without coachman, guard, passengers or anyone else. At the Bulls Head in Meriden some 5 miles from the City they had disembarked for refreshments, but the horses set off again on their own. They were hotly pursued by the coachman who was knocked down by the first horse and then run over by the coach, but amazingly suffered only minor injuries.

Perhaps the strangest story of all was reported by the *Coventry Mercury* for 18th November 1799. Between 5 and 6 am on Monday 11th, a train of fire was witnessed by several people in different areas. This was supposedly caused by a meteor, and apparently visible for at least one minute. A guard on a mail coach travelling through Woodstock in Oxfordshire said that it was as if the meteor would fall on the coach roof, and the heat was so intense that he clapped hands to his head convinced that his hair had been singed. Almost immediately the "meteor" seemed to dissolve into a blue smoke, leaving behind an overpowering smell of sulphur.

The Golden Age of Coaching

The golden age of coaching, as it was posthumously called, lasted roughly from 1820 to 1837, the year that the government authorised carrying mails by train and the London & Birmingham Railway opened. Although this was a relatively short period, it was a time of maximum efficiency in staging, with coachmen, proprietors, coach builders and all concerned at the zenith of their proficiency. It is also one of the most important periods in the history of transport and communications worldwide.

The early years of the 19th century had witnessed two of the most important advances in coaching. In 1805 (probably due to a recommendation by John Wardle, the earliest coaching amateur), springs were installed under the driver's box seat, enabling coachmen to drive for longer distances. Secondly, stages on coach routes were reduced first to 20 miles, then to 10, with fresh coachmen at intervals to enable continuous running. By the 1830s some stages were as short as 6 miles.

Concurrently there were improvements in coach building, the quality of horses and harness, the speed of coaches, coachmen and guards, the proprietors and the staff that ran the inns.

Each stagecoach route required several vehicles, with four the desirable minimum. For a daily run of about 100 miles an "up" and "down" coach were needed, with a spare at each end to cover breakdowns. So the Birmingham *Tally-Ho!* or Shrewsbury *Wonder* were not single vehicles any more than named railway trains are a single engine and carriages. To complicate matters, the same name was often used for different routes in various parts of the country. Rival proprietors on the Birmingham to London route used *Tally-Ho!* and there were *Tally-Hos!* on other routes, as you will see.

The punctuality of the stage and mail coach system in its heyday was not achieved simply by driving horses harder. In fact mails were expressly forbidden to gallop. Less knowledgeable artists than the acclaimed James Pollard (1792-1865) often depicted galloping coach horses, but this was uncommon. Coachmen did "spring" their horses, or put them to a canter up steep hills to help make the ascent or, when conditions were favourable, a coachman might gallop for a few minutes to make up time or outdistance a rival, but in general it was not necessary. Galloping meant an increase in speed that could not be maintained, and the risk to passengers, horses and coach was too great.

"Springing them".

In addition to the long and medium distance stagecoach routes there were perhaps as many coaches on the short stage system. Here slower vehicles generally pulled by two horses filled in gaps at angles and sometimes even parallel to the main coach routes.

A taste of a coach journey just before the golden age can be found in 1817 timetable of a two day journey from London to Malvern. The coach left Piccadilly at 8.30am and travelled at around 8 miles per hour to reach Oxford at 4pm. The travellers then had a 12 hour break for sight seeing, eating and sleeping before the journey resumed at 4am. At noon they reached Worcester for lunch and a two a half hour break. The coach started again at 2.30 and reached West Malvern in time for an evening meal.

It has been calculated that in 1820 a person had 1,500 opportunities every 24 hours to leave London by stagecoach, and over 40 went to Birmingham. Among the busiest roads out of London were those to Brighton, Bath and Bristol, Exeter, Birmingham, Shrewsbury and Holyhead. In 1821 journey times from Birmingham to London were cut dramatically. From the Castle and Saracen's Head Inns, Birmingham the *London Royal Union* could reach London via Coventry and Daventry in 16 hours. From the Albion Hotel Coach Office, Carrs Lane and High Street, the *Aurora* day coach to London "carrying 4 insides" and travelling via Stratford, Shipston, Woodstock, Oxford, and High Wycombe, took 15 hours to reach the Bull and Mouth Inn.

Horses were by far the most expensive part of running a coach. They were often referred to as "cattle" by those in the industry, and sometimes treated no better. But on the whole they became better looking animals as coaching progressed. This still left a lot to be desired. The term to "die in harness" comes from these times, and in the summer of 1821 about 20 horses dropped dead on a single mail coach run. It was not increased speeds which killed them, but the weight; excess loads of merchandise could often pay better than passengers. Still, great care was taken that all at least looked well, as Anthony Burgess put it - "the groomed and shining exterior of the beast, like that of the coach, often bely what lay within". Dishonest proprietors sometimes provided inferior or diseased horses for night coaches, when darkness prevented close inspection by the coachman. Stolen horses were also reserved for night runs when they were much less likely to be recognised.

Harry Sainsbury who drove the *Tantivy* between Oxford and Birmingham, always complained about the quality of the horses provided at Stratford upon Avon. The whole team was not worth £25, said Harry, and he thought they had probably belonged to Shakespeare.

Better horses were used by the more prosperous contractors, such as William Chaplin in London, whose stable of 1300 was turned over every three years. For coach work an especially fine horse was bred, the Cleveland from Yorkshire, and many of these "short legged, quick stepping cattle" were very valuable, well kept animals. Other teams were matched in colour, two teams of "four dapple, smart greys" for the Blenheim to London coach were supposed to be worth 400 guineas (£420) and £100 was said to be the price of a certain brown gelding. But the general run of horses were far cheaper. In the 1820s the average price of London horses was £50 to £45, falling to £20 to £25 elsewhere. Blemished horses might fetch £15.

In 1827 it was reckoned that it cost £25 per week to maintain a coach horse, and that they had to be replaced every three or four years. When their coaching life was over they were generally sold to traders and farmers, and most lived out their lives in relative comfort.

Though some easier country stages could get away with eight horses for a 10 mile stage, most fast coaches needed one horse per mile. Five horses (a team of four plus one spare) had to be provided to pull a coach over each 10 mile stage, and there was a coach in each direction daily, so the number of horses needed was the equivalent to the length of the stage in miles.

None of the stud of 150 horses hauling the famous Shrewsbury *Wonder* in the 1820s worked more than two hours in twenty four, a policy that was as economical as humane because they often travelled their 10 mile stages in five minutes less than the scheduled time. They were said to be worth between £25 and £30 each, and on such a fast route were rarely kept for more than four years.

According to the Duke of Beaufort, long journeys on level roads were more tiring for the horses then slightly undulateing ones. The old coachmen used to say that they preferred a big heavy horse for a hilly run, and a small, compact, quick stepping, faster little horse for a flat stage.

As the industrial revolution gathered pace, speed and efficiency had to improve to meet the growing demand for more rapid transport of passengers and light goods. Thus coaching as an industry grew dramatically. The average number of stagecoaches licensed in Britain in the period 1810-1814 was 1,133 per year. This was to grow to over 3000 in 1835, an increase of 4.7% a year. Perhaps the most rapid growth took place after the post war depression from around 1822/3.

Millions of pounds were tied up in coaches, horses and inns. Around 30,000 people were estimated to be directly employed as proprietors, coachmen and guards, clerks, bookkeepers, ostlers, porters, innkeepers and their staff. This could well be a cautious estimate; as late as 1851 the census recorded 16,839 coachmen (who were not domestic servants), guards and postboys in Great Britain.

In addition there were auxiliary industries employing coach builders, harness makers, whip and bugle makers, coach lace and fringe makers, farriers and so on. A Birmingham directory for 1830 lists 22 coach and gig builders, 46 coach furniture and harness platers, 18 coach harness makers, 6 coach lace, fringe and tassel manufacturers, and 3 coach spring makers. These included one of the few women recorded in the industry in this area; Mary Smith of 23 Coleshill Street had been in the coach building business for at least eight years from this address.

In itself the coaching industry was a significant economic force, but the system carried the commercial life blood of the country, illustrated dramatically when heavy snow crippled the network in 1836. In half the time taken thirty years earlier, letters, solicitors papers, parcels, bills of exchange, large sums of money, travellers, businessmen, politicians and farmers, were sped around the country by stagecoach.

The system often brought unexpected prosperity to strategically placed towns. In the Midlands places such as Atherstone, Coleshill, Henley in Arden, Shipston on Stour and Southam flourished. Even in established towns like Warwick, Rugby, Stratford, Worcester and Shrewsbury coaching played a significant part in the economy. One village might be said to have moved en bloc. Long before the turnpike opened from Bromsgrove to Dudley, the ancient village of Kenelmstowe near St Kenelm's church on the flanks of the Clent Hills, had lost its traditional income from pilgrims. When the turnpike opened the inhabitants moved to it and formed the village of Romsley just south of Halesowen.

Shrewsbury's role as a coaching centre was a major factor in the growth of seaside resorts in mid Wales, notably Barmouth and Aberystwyth. There were regular coaches to them in the "Bathing Season", the journey usually taking 8 or 9 hours.

Worcester also had important links with Wales, as well as London and Birmingham. By 1820 there were eight coaches to Birmingham, including a mail, and all except one of them daily. They included the *True Blue* and the *Defiance* from the Star and Garter Hotel, two light post coaches going through Bromsgrove from the Unicorn Inn, and a Royal Mail leaving the Star and Garter every night at 8 o'clock.

As well as carrying passengers, stagecoaches carried light goods of high value. So bank notes, bills of exchange, jewellery, fashionable articles such as silk haberdashery, game and some ironmongery were all regularly carried by coach. The Kidderminster to London coach often carried large amounts of needles, regardless of weight.

It was because their goods were in such urgent demand that merchants used stagecoaches, and they were prepared to pay excessive prices. It cost as much as £1 to send a small box of needles. A Birmingham linen draper, Richard Westall, reckoned that in 1832 it cost 8s 4d per cwt, compared with 5 shillings by carrier wagon, to convey his supplies from London. But generally coaches had limited space for such items. Frederick Barnes, a wholesale ironmonger in Birmingham and London, frequently had packages refused. "It has been the ruin of our business", he said.

Coachmen and guards would often bring requested items from neighbouring towns, throwing them down as they passed, and they picked up parcels in similar expert manner. Some important assignments were entrusted to coach crews; it was common for country gentlemen to send important communications to London in their care, and for farmers to send rents to distant landlords.

One consignment went astray and languished unnoticed at the Castle Inn, Birmingham. In time porters and clerks became increasingly distressed by a "strong and most disgusting effluvia". Eventually the "loathsome smell" became intolerable and was traced to a large, long box which had been there for at least two years. Inside were the remains of a corpse in an advanced stage of decay.

Corpses were a fairly common illegal cargo. At a time when there was a shortage of subjects for dissection, body snatchers masquerading as organised companies exhumed newly buried corpses for sale to London and Edinburgh teaching hospitals.

Readers may have heard of Burke and Hare in Birmingham. Sometimes these consignments would be forwarded in wooden cases as "books", or such like.

Filling the Boot.

Coaches would carry all sorts of things. In 1837 a coach from Worcester was taking convicts for transportation, when a mob of "the most desperate characters of the city" appeared hurling stones and abuse. If not for the police escort "the intention of the mob to rescue the convicts would have been effected". Further along the route another mob of about five hundred "ruffians" had assembled, but a swift detour by the coachman "disappointed them". It was common at this time to transport convicts chained to the coach, despite the understandable objections of the other passengers.

News of serious criminal offences was carried by coaches, and they were frequently a means of detection. This was particularly true of horse stealing because coach crews would usually notice horses along the road, and often they gave information. In one case two horses stolen at Lutterworth were spotted by the Leamington to Warwick coachman, who also managed to bring the thief into Aylesbury for trial.

Unlike the era of the highwayman, passengers in coaching's heyday were not robbed at the point of a gun, but discreetly as they waited at inns or aboard the coach. In 1818 the Holyhead Mail was robbed repeatedly until guard Henry Harris was brought to trial for the crime. In 1838 when a box containing £900 cash and £700 in bills vanished from a coach, James Randle, the driver and a "cad" named Worrall were suspected.

In 1822 a Birmingham coach stopped at the Swan with Two Necks in London was robbed of £7,000 from the strongbox. Five years later at Furnival's Inn, Holborn the Warwick mail was robbed of £20,000. The guard saw a man approach the coach, throw a coat across a seat as if meaning to travel, then walk away. The guard carried on with loading, putting two money parcels on a seat opposite the coat intending to lock them away when he had a minute. Moments later both parcels and coat had disappeared; the stranger must have been watching everything from a concealed position in the coachyard.

On one occasion the Birmingham *Greyhound* was robbed of £420. At Coventry it was discovered that only the valuable parcel was missing and nothing else had been touched:

> "The plan was, no doubt, deliberately laid, and the whole of the movements of the persons employed about the coach .... watched. The exact place too in which the parcel was deposited must have been ascertained by the thieves."

Despite increasingly sophisticated means of detection, coach robberies continued until the end of the coaching era. In 1839 £5,000 in notes and gold were put in a box at the rear of the Manchester - Staffordshire *Potter* . As an extra precaution, a large chain ran right around the coach and across the boot, terminating near the driver's feet. In one of the most "daring and audacious robberies" of the time, the box disappeared in the 4 miles between Macclesfield and Gosworth, the boot being completely broken open.

After about 1820 there began a great change in the coaching workforce. The pace had increased and drunkenness had, on the whole, become a thing of the past. Coachmen of the old school were vanishing as they retired or were killed, injured or sacked. The new type of coachman had better education and more temperate habits, though the older, rougher style sometimes survived away from London andrthe main routes.

The coachman was quite often a colourful, extrovert character much admired by the public. "Handsome Jack Everitt" worked various teams in Coventry. Famous on the road, he also made a considerable fortune because he knew the secrets of horse racing, the prize ring, cock fighting and other "gentlemanly" sports. Another was Tom Pinner who drove the *Little Wonder* from Birmingham to Coventry. He was a large, stout man of good humour, fond of story telling and a good driver, though not averse to racing other coachmen on the road.

There were all sorts of tricks by which the coachman and guard amused travellers. One driver could throw his whip to twist the cord around the stem of a man's pipe and remove it as he stood gazing at the coach, amazingly without harming the smoker. A similar story might relate to the same driver. Sometimes descending Hagley Hill (on the Birmingham - Kidderminster road) he was able to lasso a duck and land it in the lap of a very surprised box seat passenger.

Samuel Hayward, driver of the Shrewsbury *Wonder,* became a legend in his lifetime. There are many stories about his single minded approach to driving and introverted character. A lawyer coming to Shrewsbury for the first time noticed the steepness of the Wyle Cop and, leaning forward to touch Hayward on the arm, said "I think I'll get off". "You be damned!" came the reply. Normally sullen and silent, he must have been greatly moved to speak at all. It is said that there used to be bets amongst the passengers as to whether he would utter a single word during a journey. "What the deuce ails you?" one passenger asked, "Are you dumb man?". "Can't drive and talk too", Hayward replied.

John Mockett, a much travelled diarist, wrote of coachmen in 1834:

> "The coaches proceed at such a rapid rate, that persons not knowing the country, can get but little information unless they sit by the coachman, some of whom are very intelligent men, and much superior to the old fashioned, bluff, coarse and uncivil creatures, who drank every time they stopped, so that at the end of the journey, they were nearly tipsey."

Men often came into coaching because the money was good. The weekly wage was low at between 10 and 16 shillings, about the same as an agricultural labourer, but it was accepted by passengers and proprietors that most of the drivers' earnings would come from tips. Extracting them was called "kicking" or "shelling", and involved the coachman or guard approaching the passengers with hand outstretched uttering the prompt, "I am leaving you now sir". The usual tip was between 2 shillings and 2sh. 6d per 50 miles.

During coaching's golden age several of the new breed of coachmen were prefixed "Gentleman", because of their polite manner, elegance, origins, or perhaps all three. "Gentleman" Marsh drove the Birmingham *Crown Prince* , whilst "Gentleman" Wood, also on the Birmingham road was:

> "a handsome roguish-looking man. He wears a white hat, his boots are brilliantly polished (they were wellingtons)… his drab greycoat is faultlessly clean, and the dark blue handkerchief is daintily tied. His whiskers are carefully brushed forward and curled, the flower in his buttonhole is as fresh as if that instant plucked…" [Early wellingtons, as worn by the Iron Duke, were of leather. Rubber came later.]

Many gentleman drivers had been army officers. Working out of Birmingham were Captains Pead and Douglas on the Derby road, and Captains Warbrick and Probyn on the Cheltenham road. Captain Douglas drove the Birmingham and Sheffield Mail and was "a quiet nice coachman who after a long stage of 16 miles to Lichfield brought his team in fresh". Before entering coaching he had fought in the Peninsular War.

The typical coachman would have a ruddy complexion
and be heavily dressed in a great buttoned overcoat, a
broad brimmed hat and large boots. One 19th poet described him:

> "Twas a man robust and burly,
>   Who went coaching late and early,
> And who rarely lost his temper,
>   Or descended to a rage.
> With a joyous laugh and hearty,
>   He would drive his merry party,
> While he told full many stories
>   On his well-appointed stage."

Coachmen were changed throughout the journey, but the
guard usually remained aboard throughout, perhaps up to
24 hours without rest. Only the Post Office limited their
guards to 100 mile journeys. So his job was more arduous
than that of coachman and required a nimbler, fitter man.

The duties of the guard were to attend passengers and their
needs, sort out waybills and parcels, load and unload the
coach, and apply the skid pan brake. As a guard was supposedly the senior partner, he also had to keep the driver
from recklessness and drink, and up to time. It was the
guard's job to utter the magic word "Right" which started
the coach on its journey, prompting the coachman into
"Loose their heads!" to the ostlers.

Often a guard could play a fair tune on the coach horn or
the key bugle, and so earned good tips. Tom Botterill of
the *Tally-Ho!* was apparently unequalled in this area, and
became known as "Old Rorey" from playing his favourite
tune "Rorey o'More". He was so used to his work that he
moved around the side of the coach like a cat, even at speed,
and was always on hand with amusing anecdotes. Harry
Horton was another celebrated personality who became
well known as the crack guard on the *Patent Tally Ho!*
and a fine performer on the key bugle.

Not all day coaches ran with guards, probably because they
took up the space of a paying passenger. It was then up to
the coachman to do the guard's work.

Despite many romantic and funny stories about coachmen,
they were not always so affable. A document in the Warwick

County Records Office is titled *Penalties received from Stage Coachmen* . An entry of 29th November 1836 involves *Wonder* driver John Wilcox:

"By cash of Mr. H.F. Moore Griffiths of Birmingham one of the Clerks of the Petty Sessions there the Penalty of £5 on the conviction of John Wilcox of Birmingham Stagecoachman for having on the 19th day of October last at Birmingham used insulting and abusive language to Edward Lloyd Williamson Esquire."

Giving them a Start.

There are two more entries for coachmen fined for the same offence. The second on 7th January 1838 records a penalty of £1. 5 shillings "on the conviction of John Humphreys of Birmingham Stage Coachman."

A hazard facing many coachmen was informers. In the late 18th century there was no effective police force, and coaching accidents were increasing from overloading and careless driving. An Act of 1788 laid down the maximum number of passengers to be carried in a coach. It also decreed that half of any penalty imposed for breaking this law should go to the person who provided the information.

Increasingly complex legislation followed, dealing with luggage, lettering, licence plates and some of the sort of detail found in modern vehicle regulations. It became possible to make a living out of informing on any coach that did not meet the requirements. The informer was: "a sneaky sort of rascal, who nevertheless, performed some service for the good of the community". They were particularly disliked by coachmen, and it became oppressive when they were harassed for petty infringements of obscure rules, sometimes of the informer's invention. Even so, informers usually had the law and public sentiment on their side.

By about 1830 speed was the main concern of coaching and travel times on main routes had generally been reduced to a quarter of those in the mid 18th century. The Shrewsbury *Wonder,* for example, was scheduled to leave the Bull and Mouth at 6.30 am and from the Peacock, Islington, at 6.45. It usually arrived in Shrewsbury at 10.30 pm, 14.75 hours later and covering the 158 miles at an average speed of 10.7 miles per hour. The time allowed for stops was 80 minutes, so the average travelling seems to have been at well over 11.5 miles per hour, though it is not clear how often this was achieved. Considering that the journey had taken four days in the mid 18th century it was a huge achievement.

The *Wonder* was probably the most famous stagecoach of all. Put on in 1825 as the first "Fast Day Coach", it soon became unrivalled for punctuality. It was horsed by Sherman from the Bull and Mouth in London to St Albans and driven over this section by a coachman named Wood. From here Harry Lily took over until he met John Wilcox (mentioned earlier in connection with a fine) who drove to Birmingham. From there to Shrewsbury Sam Hayward occupied the box.

Another famous Midland coach was the Birmingham *Tally Ho!*. The name seems to have captured the imagination of proprietors throughout the country and many used it. An advertisement in *Aris's* from December 1822 describes what may well be the original *Tally Ho!* which was put on from the Nelson Hotel, High Street by W Radenhurst & Co, Birmingham and W Horne in London. The coach boasted "speed, safety, unrivalled accommodation from end to end" and travelled through Coventry to Charing Cross, London in 14 hours.

By September 1823 the proprietors had to change the name to *Independent Tally Ho!* because rivals were introducing another coach of the same name on the route. The journey had by now been cut to 13.5 hours.

By April 1827 there was another *Independent Tally Ho!* to Chester via Wolverhampton, Stafford, Eccleshall and Nantwich in 10 hours. In 1835 came the *Original Tally Ho!* from the Castle and Saracens Head Inns, and St Georges Tavern, the *Independent Tally Ho!* from the Nelson Hotel, and the *Tally Ho!* from the Swan Hotel, all leaving early in the morning and travelling the same route to London. There was also an *Eclipse Tally Ho!* and a *Patent Tally Ho!*, as well as *Tally Ho!* s to Dudley and Gloucester from the Castle and Saracens Head Inns and St Georges Tavern, to Wednesbury from the Lamp Tavern and to Wolverhampton from the Fountain, New Street.

The *Tantivy* was another famous Birmingham coach which had started running in 1832. Its route from London passed through Maidenhead, Henley, Oxford, Woodstock, Shipston on Stour, Stratford upon Avon and Henley in Arden, about 125 miles covered in 12 hours. Departing from London at 7.00 am it averaged 11 miles per hour on a good run and was once driven through its journey in a single sitting by Cracknell, its most famous coachman. In 1835 another fast day coach called the *Courier* was put on the same route to start two hours earlier.

The famed *Crown Prince* coach was running between Birmingham and London via Warwick and Leamington by 1821, and still travelled the same route in 1835. Other notable Midlands coaches included the Birmingham to London *Nimrod*, the Birmingham - Worcester *True Blue*, and the Birmingham - Liverpool *Bang Up*.

As in the late 18th century, coach names in this period gave a glimpse of the social, political and historical ideas of the time. In Coventry there were the *Lady Godiva* and *Peeping Tom* coaches, and from Birmingham a *Wellington* ran to Bristol, a *Prince of Orange* to Chester and a *Flying Dutchman* to London. The Shrewsbury to Holyhead route had a *Prince Regent*, Dudley to Birmingham an *Earle Grey*, Worcester to London a *"Mazeppa"* (after Byron's poem of that name), Kidderminster to Birmingham a *British Queen* and Wednesbury to Birmingham a *Waterloo*. A Leamington coach was called the *Liberal*.

In the early 1830s a coach journey was generally much more enjoyable than it had been twenty or thirty years before. An article in the *Evesham Journal* for 7th July 1930 entitled *Leaves from a Lady's Diary*, gives a description of a young lady's coach journey to London:

> "It was a great event in those days. She was taken to the Cross-roads on the London road, and she and her box dumped down to await the arrival of the coach. She sat on her box for some time, a very excited little maiden, for this was her first trip to London. Being stowed away inside with the other ladies she saw very little of the scenery. Oxford was the first stopping place for change of horses, and here passengers alighted to stretch their legs. At the entrance of the Mitre Hotel, the hubs of the wheels rubbed the door portals. After a very long journey, they arrived weary, worn, but by no means sad. What a journey!"

A slightly stranger tale was told by an old lady who as a schoolgirl travelled by coach from Worcester to Stourbridge. She described how the coach stopped at the Stewponey Inn (on the A449) to allow passengers to visit the nearby gibbet where Howe, the Dunsley murderer, was hanging. The sheer loneliness of the roads is illustrated by a correspondent to the *Coventry Express*, who explained how the corpse was illegally taken off for disection by a surgeon called Mr Downing. While getting it down he heard someone coming, and in panic slipped down from the gibbet and lay flat on the ground. At this point the corpse fell on him, and he had to remain still underneath it until the person passed by. He kept the skeleton hanging up in his hall joined together with wire.

Various contrivances were attempted to obtain cheaper fares on coaches. A Coventry lady told how, as a small girl, she was taken to the coach office and booked to travel to London at half price. In the morning her elder sister boarded the coach in her place. As she did so the clerk exclaimed - "Why Mrs. X - , your little girl has grown in the night", but let her go.

At the very height of coaching in the mid 1830s, fares still varied somewhat, depending on route, type of coach, and competition. Proprietors usually advertised "Reduced Fares" as in the following advertisement from *Aris's* of July 1835:

RADENHURST'S GENERAL COACH OFFICE,
NELSON HOTEL, BULL-RING.
REDUCED FARES by the NEW LECEISTER
CRITERION COACH.

EVERY MORNING AT TWELVE O'CLOCK.

Coventry, 5s. inside-2s. 6d out.
Hinckley, 7s. inside-4s. out.
Leicester, 8s. inside-4s. out.

To the GEORGE INN, Leicester, by five o'clock, in time for Coaches to Loughborough, Nottingham, Melton &c. &c.

C. RADENHURST,
JOHN GEORGE BRIGGS & Co.
Proprietors

In 1835 fares from Leamington to London on the *Tartar* and *Crown Prince* coaches were - inside 21 shillings, outside 10 shillings. The fares on coaches from Birmingham to London in the mid 1830s were around £1 and 10 shillings inside, and 16 shillings outside.

Due to its efficiency and speed, the stagecoach system was now at its absolute peak, with 3036 licensed coaches on the roads of England and Wales in 1835. From Birmingham coaches left inns like the Hen and Chickens, New Street, the Swan, High Street, the Nelson Hotel in the Bull Ring and numerous others, to over 150 destinations daily. Local services ran to West Bromwich, Bilston, Wolverhampton, Wednesbury, Darlaston, and Willenhall, Walsall, Sutton Coldfield and Lichfield, Tamworth, Atherstone, Coventry,

GENERAL COACH OFFICE,
FLEECE INN,
Dudley Street, Wolverhampton.

LONDON.

Phœnix and **Rocket**, every evening at half-past five, calls at the Hen and Chickens Hotel, Birmingham, through Oxford, Henley-on-Thames, and arrives at the George and Blue Boar, Holborn, early next morning.—The latest coach by one hour—goes direct.

Triumph, the same route, every morning at three o'clock, and arrives at the Spread Eagle, Gracechurch-street, early the same evening.

LIVERPOOL.

Triumph, every night at half-past eleven, through Chester, and arrives at the Golden Lion, Dale-street, by half-past ten next morning.

SHREWSBURY.

Salopian, every afternoon at three o'clock, through Shiffnal, Ironbridge, Colebrook Dale, and arrives at the Talbot Hotel by seven o'clock.

HOLYHEAD.

Triumph, through Shrewsbury and Bangor, every night at half-past eleven—goes direct. Meets coaches at the Talbot Hotel, Salop, for Hereford, Aberystwith, Welchpool, Newtown, and all parts of North Wales.

POTTERIES.

Hark Forward! every evening at a quarter before six, through Stafford, Stone, Lane End, Stoke, Shelton, Hanley, to the Legs of Man, Burslem, by half-past ten the same night.

BIRMINGHAM.

Active, day coach, every morning at a quarter before nine.

Salopian, every morning at eleven o'clock, to the King's Head, Worcester-street.

Hark Forward! at twelve o'clock, to the King's Head, Worcester-street, in time for Leamington, Warwick, Coventry, and Leicester coaches.

Favourite, every afternoon at a quarter before three, in time for Worcester, Bromsgrove, &c., &c.

Phœnix, every evening at half-past five, to the Hen and Chickens Hotel, in time for the Bristol Mail.

Tally-ho! every evening at a quarter before eight. This coach renders great accommodation, being the only conveyance after six o'clock.

Triumph, every morning at three o'clock, to the Hen and Chickens Hotel, in time for the Stamford and Leamington mails.

BRIDGNORTH.

Every morning at half-past ten, and returns in time for Birmingham and London coaches.

Coach Timetable for 1830

Solihull and Knowle, Warwick and Leamington, Henley
in Arden and Stratford upon Avon, Bromsgrove and
Worcester, Stourbridge and Kidderminster.

In Leamington over 30 coaches a day departed from its inns.
Warwick sent 12 coaches daily to Birmingham, including the
Crown Prince and *Bang Up*, two to Liverpool and six to Coventry, including the locally renowned *Shakespeare* . There
were also departures for London, Cambridge, Cheltenham,
Oxford and Worcester, all from coaching inns standing a few
yards apart round the market place. It must have been madly
busy, with the clatter of hooves and wheels, shouts of coachmen and guards, and the frantic bustle of ostlers and stable
boys as they tried to get coaches away on time. This scene
was repeated up and down the country during the golden age
of coaching. But, if you looked hard enough, on the horizon
you could just make out the faintest tinge of rising smoke.

Putting to the Team.

Coaching Inns
and Coach Proprietors

The operation of the stagecoach system depended largely
on the inns, which were usually owned wholly or partly by
coach proprietors.   In the golden years of coaching, inns
were efficiently run, worked day and night and were the
foundation on which the whole road transport system stood.
Besides providing passenger accommodation and meals, inns
were the staging posts and terminals for all coach services.
The innkeeper would often be directly involved in coaching
as a partner in a coach service or a contractor, employed
to "horse" a coach over a particular stage. Many inns had
facilities for "posting", or hiring out of post chaises,
and some had upwards of four hundred horses on hand.

The keeper of a big inn supervised a complex organisation
of cooks, waiters, kitchen maids, hairdressers, ostlers,
stable boys and chaise drivers. They were often notable
figures in the local community, to which they brought trade
and much indirect employment. In some lesser towns where
there was no special local industry and little market trade,
the road network and the inns were economically essential.

The inn was no new thing, the innovation of the coaching era lay in their proliferation and being drawn into an
organised structure. Inns developed gradually from the reign
of Elizabeth I and reached their peak of affluence when Victoria was crowned in 1837. Initially they had been built by
mediaeval monks to cater for pilgrims and travellers. John
Twyning and his monks built the New Inn at Gloucester in
the 14th century to cater for two hundred of the pilgrims
going to the shrine of Edward II (1307-1327). The George
& Pilgrims in Glastonbury's main street was built by Abbott
John Selwood at about the same time. After the Reformation
this tradition of hospitality passed to commercial owners.

The true coaching inn prospered for only thirty or forty
years and was created in London, with much of its income
coming from the mail. New inns were built for the business,
but many families had town or country houses that could be
modified. Probably it was when these were taken over that
painting of inn signs with the arms of the former owners
became the fashion. It certainly seems to have been

introduced in the 18th century, and was perhaps thought to add a certain class to the premises. Such signs would have been of little use earlier. Inns had pictorial signs for those unable to read, but who could recognise such badges as the bear & ragged staff of the Earls of Warwick, or the blue boar of the Earls of Oxford. The inn sign was significant because it linked the landlord with the gentleman, rather than the tradesman, and imitated the signs displayed by nobleman at their town houses.

The 19th century coaching inn needed certain facilities to operate. Horses had to be stabled and shod, harness needed constant care, and most important, passengers had to be fed and accommodated on overnight stops. Many inns were re-built towards the end of the 18th century to provide large numbers of bedrooms, ample public rooms, stabling, repair sheds, and usually a through access from front to back.

The efficiency of inns in providing fresh horses and catering for passengers determined whether timetables were fulfilled. At important inns where the men knew their jobs well, two minutes was enough to change coach horses, and sometimes fifty seconds. It brings to mind the pit stops in Formula One motor racing. However, the incessant pursuit of speed by stagecoaches actually hit the inns hard, as many coaches ran day and night to improve times and did not need overnight accommodation. Occasionally the innkeeper would bribe a coachman and guard to delay longer than their schedule allowed in the hope of extra custom.

The coaching industry often brought work where there had been little or none. New inns spread rapidly throughout the country, usually converted from mansions, large houses and farms. Frequently those in isolated places but beside main roads were extended and generated a whole new area of industry in and around them.

Although the great London inns, such as the Swan With Two Necks and the Bull & Mouth, were the main links in the coaching network, major provincial towns also had important inns.

During the early days of coaching in Birmingham the Swan (long demolished) was the town's main inn. In fact it is the only one shown on a 1731 plan of the town centre, where it appears in "High Town", later High Street, close to the junct-

George Hotel, Lichfield

Wolsley Arms between Stafford and Rugeley

Swan Hotel, Coleshill

White Swan, Henley in Arden

The Talbot, Stourbridge

ion with New Street. This was where Nicholas Rothwell's Birmingham Stage Coach started on 24th May 1731. The Swan was later rebuilt so that horses could be stabled, and for the first time an arch gave access from the street to the yard.

The Hen & Chickens (formerly the High Tower), stood not far from the present Odeon cinema and soon began to rival the Swan. Judging from the announcement of a "Flying Coach" in Aris's *Birmingham Gazette* of 1742, the inn seems to have been run by Mr Francis Cox. An item in the same paper on 2nd December 1743 announced its sale - "to the best Bidder, on Monday 19th December, instant, at the Dwelling-House of Francis Cox, 'The Angel and Hen & Chickens'". To the successor of this inn, the New Street Hotel, came some of most eminent men of their time, including Thomas De Quincey.

Birmingham's oldest inn is the Old Crown which still stands in High Street, Deritend at the corner of Heath Mill Road. Built in 1368 by a wealthy merchant, it was probably the town's first coaching inn around 1700, when Richard Dickson and his wife Anne were owners and landlords.

In Birmingham during the heyday of coaching, the best known of these busy, noisy establishments were still the Swan and the Hen & Chickens. But there were many others, such as the Nelson on the Bull Ring, which had changed its name from the Dog because it stood opposite a recent statue of Nelson, the St George's Tavern, the Castle on the corner of Castle Street and the Albion at the junction of High Street and Carrs Lane. There was also the Saracen's Head in Bull Street, near the junction with Temple Street and backing onto Old Square. Not one of them remains.

In the important Midlands coaching town of Shrewsbury, the best inn was certainly the Lion in Wyle Cop. It was mainly the creation of Robert Lawrence who moved there from the Raven in 1780, along with his flourishing stage-coach business. Under him the Lion became one of the most acclaimed coaching inns in the country and dominated the trade for over fifty years. One observer wrote:

"no house upon any of the great roads stands in higher estimation, having a constant influx of the finest families of the kingdom."

There was intense rivalry between the Lion, the Talbot, the Raven & Bell and the Britannia. Considerable areas of central Shrewsbury were given over to stabling.

The Lion was built in the 1770s by the lawyer John Ashby who lived in the next house, and was intended as a social centre for the country gentry. When Robert Lawrence arrived he had the Holyhead Road diverted from its old Chester route to run through Shrewsbury, a classic example of how much an inn could influence a road. The achievement is commemorated on his tombstone in St Julian's churchyard. In 1825 the Lion was owned by the renowned Isaac Taylor, who with Edward Sherman of London put on the Shrewsbury *Wonder*. Today the Lion is one of the few great coaching inns left.

In Ludlow the building in Old Street which is now a library has a Regency facade, a rarity in the town. This was added when the building was a coaching inn known as the Golden Lion.

In Southam near Leamington, the recently closed Craven Arms was the main coaching inn, with about eighty horses always on hand. Trade was so brisk that the landlord built six small cottages (known as "the saucy six" after their occupants) to house additional ostlers. The inn burned down in 1742 but was soon rebuilt to flourish again. Southam had well over a dozen inns at one time or another in the coaching era. They included the King's Head, where Napoleon III is supposed to have stayed; it is now a private house - "The Warren".

At Alcester west of Stratford on Avon, the Angel Inn was one of the two main coaching inns. Queen Victoria stayed there when she was Princess of Kent and it furnished the wedding breakfasts of the Princess of Wales and Princess Alexandria of Denmark. The Angel also housed the ghost of a Captain Richard Hill. It went out of business many years ago and the building was converted into two houses.

Alcester's other main coaching inn was the Swan in Swan Street, which still functions as a pub. To cater for the growing coach trade the original building was demolished in the early 18th century and the present building erected. In the late 1790s the inn was renovated by its owner, Mr John Stevens of Cold Comfort Lane Farm. The Swan had an important role in the coaching trade of the area, being

on the main route from London to Kidderminster. It was
also the main local terminal for coaches heading for important towns like Birmingham, Stratford and Evesham.

The Bath Hotel in Leamington Spa was opened in 1786 by
William Abbots on the corner of Bath and Smith Streets as
the New Inn. It survived until 1950 when it became a super-
market. The Copps Hotel which stood on the eastern corner
of High Street extending into Court Street has also been demolished. This big hotel built in 1827 by Michael Copps had
one hundred beds, stables for fifty horses and stands for forty
carriages. Another coaching inn was the Bedford Hotel on The
Parade. It was opened on 25th October 1811 under the owner-
ship of a Mr and Mrs Williams, formerly a butler and house-
keeper. The site now houses a Midland Bank.

Other well known Midland coaching inns included the White
Swan at Henley in Arden, which is happily and completely
still in business as a pub. In Stratford upon Avon were the
White Lion, Henley Street and Red Horse in Bridge Street.
Lichfield had the George and the Swan in Bird Street which
are now hotels. The Craven Arms (formerly White Bear) in
High Street, Coventry has gone, whilst the Swan in High
Street, Coleshill is a hotel. The Dun Cow at Dunchurch has
recently reopened as a pub after a period of closure. This
was where Robert Stephenson met his father, George, for a
dinner to celebrate completion of the Kilsby Tunnel and the
London & Birmingham Railway; an ominous celebration for
for coaching. In Warwick the George Inn is a building society and dress shop, and the Castle Hotel has been replaced
by Woolworth's. Worcester's Star & Garter and Hop Pole
stood in Foregate Street, but have gone.

Isolated country inns were more dependent on road travel
than those in towns. They often stood at important junctions
or on lonely stretches of turnpike because of the need for
a staging post on a particular coach route. The same is true
of inns in small villages. Advertisements for their sale or
letting usually noted as a main detail the route on which
they stood. Some stood above or below a steep hill, such
as Broadway Hill in the Cotswolds, because there was need
for a place where horses could be watered and extra ones
attached or detached.

Many of the factors which affected the siting of country
coaching inns are often not evident today. They are left

without a context, seemingly irrational points in a vanished system. On some of the main country routes small clusters of inns could be found, and with a few adjoining cottages, blacksmith's and wheelwright's shops, would have formed hamlets almost wholly sustained by the road system.

There are numerous stories about the English inn, not all complimentary. Charles Dickens's memories were not of the "good tempered smiling barmaid" mentioned by some, but of the tap waiter at the Golden Cross, Birmingham. A quarter hour before the *Highflyer* was due to leave he asked for a hot brandy and water;

> "The first stroke of six peals from St Martin's Church steeple just as you take the first sip of the boiling liquid. You find yourself at the booking office in two seconds, and the tap waiter finds himself much comforted by your brandy and water, in about the same period."

Two sailors on the Birmingham - London *Tantivy* were not as easily intimidated. When the guard sounded his horn at the Star in Oxford, they dashed out boldly with a fowl and a loaf of bread. Despite protest from the waiter they ate the food they had paid for in the coach.

W E Gladstone (1809-1898), the Prime Minister, was also an author. In a letter to the editor of a book, *Old and New Birmingham* he wrote:

> "My recollections of the casual hours in Birmingham are much less pleasant than those of my visit last year (1877). The coach inns were bad. The times of stopping chosen with reference to anything rather than the comfort of the passengers. I have repeatedly been turned out of the Liverpool coach, the *Aurora,* I think, at 4 o'clock on a winter's morning, sometimes in the frost or snow, and offered breakfast, for which this was the only time allowed; while the luggage was charged upon a barrow. Behind this barrow we mournfully trudged along the streets to the other hotel; Castle, or Albion, or Hen and Chickens, from which the sister coach was to start for the south. Such was in those days the measure of comfort deemed necessary for travellers ..."

The Hen & Chickens in Birmingham does not seem to have been to the liking of Thomas De Quincey, who commented on one of his stays:

"as to the noise, never did I sleep at that enormous Hen and Chickens ... Till 2 or 3 I was kept awake by those who were retiring."

Despite these reports, not all contemporary accounts of the English inn were as bad. The Frenchman, de Haussez, wrote:

"In many ... larger towns they are magnificent, and ... good and well supplied in the smallest. In the greatest part ... servants are in livery, and in all, their attendance is prompt and respectable."

But on the whole the general impression seems more negative. John Byng was scathing about Warwickshire inns, finding only the Swan at Merevale "tolerable". According to some writers, innkeepers left much to be desired. "Nimrod" (pseudonym of the sports writer Charles James Apperley (1770-1843)) wrote:

"English innkeepers are for the most part shamelessly indifferent to the comforts of coach passengers and ought to be shown up oftener than they are."

Apart from their role in coaching, the larger inns performed other functions; roles later taken up by public halls, court rooms and theatres. Before offices were common, businessmen met in inns, coroners held inquests in them, the parish vestry met there, and official bodies such as turnpike trusts used them for their assemblies. They were sometimes the venue for magistrates, Members of Parliament, and sales and auctions

In the evenings inns became centres for social life, with balls, parties and entertainment by travelling showmen. Throughout the whole twenty four hours coaches would be coming and going. Inns were the first place in a town or village to hear national or local news, and all the mail came through them.

The White Lion in Henley Street, Stratford upon Avon was a good example of such an inn, with a reputation as one of the leading establishments on the London - Birmingham road. It was a focal point for local affairs from the sale of theatre tickets to committee meetings, such as those of the Shottery Enclosure Committee in 1786-7. Because of the excellent coaching service at the White Lion, its proprietor John Payton was running the town's post office by 1779.

Stagecoaches were operated by proprietors, but what they usually owned was a coaching service and some horses. The actual vehicles were hired from coachmasters, much as modern businesses lease plant and cars. Many coach proprietors were also contractors who horsed and operated mail coaches for the Post Office. The majority were innkeepers, thus having an additional source of revenue, and some of the most successful ones had more than one inn.

Horsing coaches was always the most difficult and expensive part of the business. Even the bigger coaching contractors or proprietors were in the power of innkeepers on their routes, who were paid an annual fee to provide suitable horses. In areas where there were many inns contractors could negotiate the best terms. But if an isolated inn had complete control over a section of road the innkeeper could charge what he wished.

The coaching industry came to be dominated by a handful of proprietors based in London. They were William Chaplin, Edward Sherman, Benjamin Worthy Horne, Mrs Ann Nelson of the Bull Inn, Aldgate, Robert Nelson, and Mrs Ann Mountain of the Saracen's Head, Snow Hill (London). However, there were also successful and well known provincial proprietors, such as William Waddell in Birmingham and Isaac Taylor in Shrewsbury.

William Chaplin, the most famous of all coach proprietors, was the son of a Rochester coachman. He built up a huge business that by 1837 was running about two hundred coaches around the country. He began as a horse dealer then graduated to running coaches from his famous London inn, The Swan with Two Necks. Eventually he owned five London inns and between fifteen hundred and eighteen hundred horses and employed two thousand people. He supplied horses for half the London mails on the first stage out and the last stage in.

Chaplin's main rival was Edward Sherman, proprietor of the Shrewsbury *Wonder*. Sherman had agreed with the turnpike trusts to pay tolls for this coach monthly rather than stop at the gates, giving a keen advantage in speed. Sherman was able to compete with Chaplin because in 1823 he took over the Bull & Mouth in St Martins le Grand, so he was operating opposite the GPO. He also ran coaches from the Oxford Arms, Newgate, London, where his chief business was freight. Most

of his coaches ran north and north-west, and in his heyday he
had nine daily to Birmingham, his speciality being the fast
day coach.

Another competitor was Benjamin Worthy Horne who was
involved in running a rival coach to Shrewsbury to drive
the *Wonder* off the route.   Horne had three coaching inns,
including the Golden Cross in what is now Trafalgar Square.
Apparently he once forced a rival coach out of business by
buying up all the available horses at a certain stage. Horne
horsed five of the London mails to the south and west, sometimes in partnership with other London proprietors. His well
known coaches included the *Independent Tally Ho!* to Birmingham, the Liverpool *Umpire* and the Bedford *Times.*

Birmingham's foremost man in the business was William
Waddell, son of a London oil merchant. In the 1790s he
formed a business connection with a Mr Piper at The Castle
Inn, High Street, and before long came to manage his posting
business. In 1796 Waddell applied successfully to operate a
mail coach service from Birmingham to Walsall, which began
on 21st October of that year. When Piper died in 1802 Waddell took over the Castle. Two years later he leased the Hen
& Chickens, and by 1819 around thirty coaches daily were
leaving its yard for all parts of the country.

By 1830 Waddell was in possession of both the Hen & Chickens and the Swan, and with his son Thomas he continued to
develop his flourishing business. Elizier Edwards wrote that
during Waddell's time at the Hen & Chickens the:

> "... posting and coaching trade attached to the place
> grew to a business of enormous magnitude and his
> name...became a household word..."

Waddell remained a leading figure in Birmingham's coaching
business until his death in 1836.

Isaac Taylor who owned the famous Lion in Shrewsbury came
from an innkeeping family. His father had kept the Haygate
(otherwise Falcon) at Wellington, which his brother took over
in 1838. Another brother kept the Jerningham Arms, a coaching inn at Shifnal. Taylor was not actually landlord at the Lion
but restricted his affairs to the coaching business, with which
he combined farming at Monkmoor. Thomas Kenyon said of
him in 1842 that he had:

"so highly distinguished himself in this county, not
only as a coach proprietor, but as an agriculturalist,
and...he entitled himself in both capacities, to the high
esteem in which he is generally held...Such a character
for regularity the coach (i.e. the *Wonder*) could never
have obtained without good horses, good coachmen
and good tackle, and they were indebted for these to
the coach proprietor. Mr Taylor was one of the first
to accommodate the public in this excellent manner.

Isaac Taylor's grave lies outside St Julian's church a short
distance from the Lion.

Occasionally a coach might be organised by local tradesmen
who felt the lack in the ordinary services. The fishmongers
of Bristol, for example, started a Bristol - Exeter coach in
1821, and Oxford interests put on a coach around this time.

Proprietors were often seen by the public as making money at
the expense of their safety. After an accident on the Birmingham *Eclipse* a furious correspondent had some recommend-
ations for Mr Waterhouse, "who is so large a gainer by the
use, and one might say, abuse, of these public carriages".
Some proprietors did not seem to care. When the Hereford -
Chester mail went over in 1828 the passengers complained
to the owners:

"on the impropriety of putting dangerous horses to a
public conveyance, [but he] behaved with the greatest
insolence, saying, if they did not like it they might
leave the coach, as there were other passengers to take
their places."

Antagonism and bitter rivalries between proprietors horsing
coaches on the same route was fairly common. In the Midlands it occurred on various routes, but particularly on the
Holyhead and the London to Birmingham roads, where the
various *Tally-Ho!* coaches travelled at the same time.

Some writers on the subject claim that Mrs Ann Mountain
of the Saracen's Head, Snow Hill, London established the
original *Tally-Ho!* in 1823, and fought against the competition of a later *Tally-Ho!* put on by Benjamin Horne and W
Radenhurst. A series of advertisements in Aris's *Birmingham
Gazette* seem to disprove this. The first is from December
1822:

BIRMINGHAM TO LONDON
THE TALLY-HO! DAY COACH,
THROUGH COVENTRY.

SPEED, safety, unrivalled accommodation from end to end, and the nearest road, are leading features of this coach. Assured as the Proprietors are, that an atom of practice is worth a volume of idle profession, and that in proportion as they serve and accommodate the Public, so in proportion a benefit results to themselves.

This Safety Coach exceeds in expedition every other day coach from Birmingham to London, and the Proprietors are also attentive that their passengers shall be reasonably and comfortably accommodated on the road. Diligence and despatch in the care and delivery of parcels will be a prominent point of their attention.

And for the further accommodation of the public, the TALLY-HO! leaves the NELSON HOTEL (late the Dog Inn) Birmingham, every morning at seven o'clock (except Sunday, on which day it leaves at six o'clock as heretofore), and will arrive at the GOLDEN CROSS, Charing Cross, London, at nine o'clock the same evening; at each of which Hotels will be found reasonable and comfortable accommodation.

The above Coach calls at the Three Cups, Aldersgate-street, and Cross Keys, Wood Street; where passengers are booked, and all parcels for the City are left for delivery.

FARES AS CHEAP as per OTHER COACHES.
Parcels 1s each - Packages 1d per lb.

Performed by
W. RADENHURST and Co. Birmingham,
W. HORNE and Co. London.

who will not be accountable for any kind of luggage or parcels, above £5 value, unless entered and paid for acordingly.

NB. Passengers and Parcels booked at the above offices to all parts of the kingdom.

In 1823 Mrs Mountain and other proprietors were also advertising in *Aris's*. They announced the fiction that the *Tally-Ho!* had been "removed [at the London end] from the Golden Cross... to the Saracen's Head", and that it now departed (at a quarter to seven - not seven o'clock as advertised by Horne) not from the Nelson Hotel, as Horne had stated, but from the Castle Hotel and St George's Tavern, High Street (Birmingham). Mountain and Co also advised potential customers to "not apply to the Golden Cross... or to the Nelson, Birmingham, for the *Tally-Ho!* " but:

HARK FORWARD

to the Saracen's Head, London, Castle Hotel and St. George's Tavern, Birmingham, Castle and Craven Arms, Coventry, where they will join the REAL TALLY-HO!!! and after the chase, receive the best Accommodation at moderate Charges.

What this all seems to show is that Mountain and Co had purloined the name *Tally-Ho!* for their own coach. It ran the same route as the original but left a quarter of an hour earlier in the morning to beat it to London.

Horne and Radenhurst's understandably irate reply to this scheming was also published in *Aris's:*

INFORMATION AND CAUTION
To Coach Passengers and the Public generally.
TALLY-HO!

THE INDEPENDENT Day Coach to London, through Coventry, in 13 1/2 hours, leaves the
NELSON HOTEL,
Birmingham, every morning at seven o'clock, as usual.

The friends of this Coach will observe, that the decided preference given to THE INDEPENDENT since it has commenced running, owing to the steadiness of its travelling,   has already galled the Proprietors of the new coach that they have descended to the meanness of pasting their bills over those of THE INDEPENDENT, and by that contemptible trickery build a hope of mis-

leading the Public by imposing upon them the
fiction of the "Tally-ho Removed."

RADENHURST and Co. Birmingham,
HORNE and Co. London.
Proprietors.

Despite being first on the scene with the original *Tally-Ho!*,
Radenhurst and Horne changed the name of their coach to the
Independent Tally-Ho! to avoid confusion. They had also
managed in just a couple of months to cut their journey time
by half an hour. In 1827 they were still running the *Independent Tally-Ho!* from the Nelson Hotel, but leaving at
6am, while Mountain's *Tally-Ho!* was still departing from
the Castle Hotel at 6.45. Both coaches ran until the end
of the coaching era.

There were many heavy expenses involved in the coaching
industry, so few proprietors made fortunes and many went
bankrupt. Horses were the main expense, but there were also
road tolls, duty to the government, coach hire, and the wages
of coachmen and guards. Horne claimed in 1827 that the most
any contractor earned that year was a mere £4.10 shillings.
Mrs Mountain's son Peter stated a similar figure for individual stagecoach profits - "I should think...very few coaches
average £4 take the year round". Many proprietors, like mail
contractors, lost considerable sums. Even as early as 1827
William Chaplin commented:

"I have not a shadow of a doubt that, were the coaching
account of the nation kept regularly, the whole is decidedly a loss...and the public have the turn."

Things were usually much worse for the many country proprietors who supplied horses for coaches in remote and largely
unprofitable areas. Many were making substantial losses by
the 1830s and often subsidised their activities with farm
profits.

It is even possible, as Harry Hanson has suggested, that town
proprietors like Chaplin, Horne and Sherman were working at
a loss long before the railways appeared. However, they were
astute businessmen who had made considerable sums from their
various inns and coaches, and it is hard to imagine them operating at a loss for too long. Whatever the financial reality
coaches continued to run and proprietors continued to horse
them; the system still seemed to be working.

Twilight Years

Use of steam power instead of horses began in earnest with the opening of the Stockton & Darlington Railway in 1825. During the years 1823-38 steam powered road carriages were tested and occasionally used. A well known case is Charles Dance's attempt in 1832 to run a steam carriage travelling at about 10 miles per hour from London to Birmingham.

On the canals steam navigation produced average speeds of 6 or 7 miles an hour, and even that moderate pace was greater than that of the earliest tests with locomotives on railways. Speeds increased steadily, but early railways were often no faster than the crack stage coaches.

Warwickshire's first railway was horse drawn and intended to serve rather than compete with the canal network. The Stratford & Moreton Railway Act was passed in 1821, and the 16 mile line opened in 1826 between the canal basin at Bancroft, Stratford upon Avon across the county to Moreton in Marsh, with a branch to Shipston on Stour 7 miles north-east.

John Restrick, a West Midlands iron founder, engineered the line at about £33,500. Viscount Dudley was one of the Company's main shareholders and promoters, so that coal from his Black Country mines could be carried on the Stratford Canal

The brick viaduct over the Avon at Stratford
carried The Stratford & Moreton Railway.

and distributed in south-west Warwickshire and the northern Cotswolds. Meanwhile, stone, lime and various agricultural products were carried northwards.

In October 1829 Stephenson's *Rocket* won the Rainhill trials for a locomotive to be used on the forthcoming Liverpool & Manchester Railway. On 15th September 1830 the line was opened - the first in the world built for passengers as well as freight. The railway age had begun, and the beginning was rather ominous. At the opening the Liverpool MP and President of the Board of Trade, William Huskisson, did not or could not heed the shouted warning, "Mr Huskisson, Sir, do not stir." He was knocked down by the *Rocket* and died soon after.

Even after the opening of the railway, public, and to a great extent railway opinion, was that railways would deal with freight, and stagecoaches would continue to carry passengers. The idea did not last long.

Still, in the early days of the railways coach proprietors were not too worried, believing that rail travel was far too dangerous to lure away their passengers. If a coach turned over, they argued, the worst that would usually happen was a broken limb or two; if a train turned over death was inevitable. "Nimrod", writing at this time, agreed: "Is not the rate of 10 miles in an hour with safety preferable to 20, with awful risk to life and limb". There had been similar reactions to the early stagecoaches.

The *Birmingham Advertiser* for 10th October 1833 summed up the main disadvantage of rail compared with road; above all it would require the construction of an entirely new network of routes. Detractors pointed out the discomforts of early trains. First Class on the railway was very like sitting in a coach except there were six passengers inside compared to four on the mails. Second Class consisted of an open carriage with an awning to protect passengers from rain, snow, red hot cinders and smoke. Travelling Third Class meant standing in an open truck. Heavy jolting from rails laid on granite slabs had to be endured by everyone, as did the continuous and deafening clatter. Tunnels were especially unpleasant. It was thought for a while that trains could not run in severe frosts because the wheels would not grip the rails. But initial problems of adhesion were soon overcome.

Popular opposition to the new railways was much in evidence. The country's landowners berated the evils of gridironing of the country with lines, and canal interests, turnpike trusts and coach proprietors were beginning to see dangers. It was also feared that if railways put coaches out of business, agriiculture would decline because of collapse of the market for horses and fodder. This in particular is why railway companies were made to pay outrageous prices for land. Many big land developers had men on guard day and night to stop levels and measurements being taken on their property.

Every little railway failure raised coaching spirits, but by 1837 it was clear that coaching was in serious danger. Opening of a new railway line on a coach route resulted almost instantly in coaches being taken off. Even in 1832 the Liverpool & Manchester Railway caused the end of twenty eight coaches, a loss of revenue of £8,384 per year.

The first significant railway built in the Midlands was the Grand Junction, opened in 1837, which linked Birmingham with Liverpool and Manchester. The first train ran from Birmingham (Vaux Hall) to Liverpool on this line on 4th July of that year; it was extended to Curzon Street on 19th November 1838.

On 13th July 1837, just nine days after the opening of the Grand Junction, the Post Office received a letter from the people of Leek in Staffordshire. They complained that on opening of the railway the mail coach between London and Manchester had been taken off. The London mail bags were being carried from the railway at Whitmore, 17 miles away, by mail cart; letters from Manchester and Nottingham were being taken by postboys to meet a mail coach at Buxton. Letters had to be posted three hours earlier, and both mail cart and postboy were less reliable than the coach. The Post Office pointed out that it was not through their insistence that the mail coach had been removed. The contractors had told them that as they could no longer secure passengers after the opening of the railway, they could not maintain the mail coach.

The Grand Junction saw off four other mail coaches: Birmingham to Liverpool, London to Liverpool, Birmingham to Manchester, and Knutsford to Manchester. To replace them the railway provided "mail coaches" on its trains, and to places served by rail they offered a much quicker service.

But towns on former mail coach routes with no railway must have found things as difficult as the people of Leek.

On 9th April 1838 there was another major blow to the coaching industry with the opening of the London to Birmingham Railway all the way from Euston to Curzon Street, except for a section between Denbigh Hall (Fenny Stratford) and Rugby. The gap was due to work on the difficult Kilsby Tunnel south of Rugby.

At Fenny Stratford was a minor country inn called the Pig & Whistle, and when the railway was halted there a temporary roadside station was built. The Pig & Whistle was immediately elevated to the status of Denbigh Hall. From here passengers from London were carried by coach the 38 miles to Rugby to meet the Birmingham train. The arrangement continued until 17th September 1838 when the line was finished, and within weeks Denbigh Hall lapsed into obscurity.

In 1838 Parliament authorized the carrying of mails by rail. The coaches put up a vigorous fight to keep them and coachmen had to be threatened with the treadmill as punishment for furious driving. The first railway mail had been in 1830 from Liverpool to Manchester, but by late 1838 mail was already being sorted on the London to Birmingham train.

On 22nd May 1838 the Post Office announced:

"The Mails to Holyhead, Liverpool and Carlisle will be dispatched tonight for the first time by the London to Birmingham Railway. The coaches are to be drawn by horses to the terminus at Euston Square, and there to be placed on trucks and so run on the railway, retaining their coachmen, guards, passengers etc., and only requiring horses when they reach the end of the railway to proceed on their respective journeys."

Early mail trains ran to timebills almost indistinguishable from those used by mail coaches, and early trains followed coaching practice in many other ways. Carriages were shaped like stagecoaches, they had names such as *Despatch* and *Antelope*, they carried a guard, passengers (as well as guards) could travel outside, and luggage could be stacked on the roof.

By 1839 virtually all the long distance mails had been taken off and transferred to the faster and cheaper railways. In November 1842 the mail from Worcester to Ludlow which had run for almost half a century made its last journey. Two years later on 1st August 1844 the *Worcester Herald* carried the following report :

"A Mourning Coach

On Monday, a large concourse of persons assembled at Stoke's Croft to witness the last appearance of the North Mail. At the usual time, the ancient vehicle made its appearance, but the cheerful note of the guard's bugle, and the encouraging crack of the coachman's whip were no longer its accompaniments. In honour of the melancholy occasion, the horse's heads were surmounted by hearse-like plumes, while the coachman, guard and ostler (its only passengers) were decked in all the funereal habitments of woe. The north mail is now conveyed by rail."

Two other Midland railways opened in the early 1840s. The Birmingham & Gloucester (via Bromsgrove and the Lickey Incline) opened as far as Camp Hill on 17th December 1840 and was extended to Curzon Street in August of the next year. The Birmingham & Derby Junction Railway opened to Lawley Street Station on 10th February 1842.

Despite the obvious success of railways, some of the coaching fraternity were not giving up easily. In a magnificent show of defiance on a day in 1838, the Shrewsbury *Wonder* left London at the same time as the Birmingham train and actually reached its destination first. But that performance was never repeated

Some coaches tried to continue by using fewer horses or reducing fares. In 1839 Mountain and Sherman were offering fares of £1.10 shillings inside and 10 shillings outside on coaches from Birmingham to London. Their advert was also at pains to make it clear that - "the mails and coaches from their establishments continue to run between this town and London heretofore". Radenhurst also advertised reduced fares from the Nelson Hotel Coach Office, Spiceal Street, and the Great Western Coach Office, New Street. He was running two London coaches, as well as the appropriately named *Defiance* to Bath and Bristol. Waddell and Bretherton were still advertising four coaches daily between Birmingham and London in 1839, but this was ill advised in a year when coaches were taken off daily.

Isaac Taylor of the Lion Inn, Shrewsbury, announced at this time that fares on the *Wonder* to London were being reduced, and that when the coach arrived in Birmingham passengers had a choice of remaining on it or joining a train for the rest of the journey.

By early 1839 four coaches from the Lion, two from the George, and one from the coach office on Wyle Cop were travelling to Birmingham to connect with the trains. Only the *Royal Mail* and *Greyhound* still ran to London, probably to cater. for intermediate towns without a station. But in late 1840 they were profiting from all the publicity given to railway accidents.

> "recent numerous and fatal accidents on railways have had the effect in Shrewsbury at least of bringing into favour the comparatively safer mode of travelling by the roads in good carriages with careful drivers and swift horses. Since the announcement of half-a-dozen railway accidents in one week, with a loss of seven lives, the *Greyhound* coach from Shrewsbury to London has been as full as the old *Wonder* used to be a few years ago... After all, though the railway speed of 25 miles per hour does carry a man on very swiftly, a less rapid but more safe mode of transport must be appreciated by those who have no particular relish for broken bones or sudden death."

Details of railway accidents littered the newspapers, just as coaching ones had done a few years earlier. *Aris's Birmingham Gazette* for Monday 22nd January 1838 described a "fearful accident" on the railway. This involved the Grand Junction Railway Second Class train from Liverpool to Birmingham. Just outside Darlaston the train hit a horse which had strayed onto the line from a paddock:

> "The shock was so violent that it threw the train off the line, the engine and tender breaking from the carriages and plunging down the embankment. At the foot of the declivity, the concussion threw the fireman, James Hewitt off the tender, which turned over and crushed him to death..."

Although seen on a national scale the decline of coaching seems dramatically sudden, the changeover from road to rail was not an overnight occurrence. To build a railway system linking the main towns in Britain took twenty years or more. Change from road to rail was unrelenting but slow, as money had to raised, Parliament persuaded to pass an Act, routes had to be surveyed and track laid.

Stagecoaches were taken off as the inter city links developed, but did not disappear instantly. Vehicles were still being built and even put on as normal on some short or out of the way routes. It was not until the 1860s or even later that many remote areas of the country were connected with the rail system, and some never were. In the intervening years coach operators often demonstrated great enterprise in providing links with the railway.

Cooperation between railway companies and coach owners increased during the 1840s. In Shrewsbury for example, coaches like the *Wonder*, *Stag*, *Original Salopian* and *Young Prince* often adjusted their schedules to match train times at Birmingham. All were taken off when trains started to run between Birmingham and Shrewsbury.

Isaac Taylor saw advantages and opportunities in the opening of the railways despite their threat to coaching. He worked with them to offer connections at Birmingham before Shrewsbury's railway was open. With the opening of the Shrewsbury and Chester line he started a bus service between the station and the Lion, and secured the valuable agency for delivering parcels brought in by rail.

Many large coach proprietors went into railways as directors or shareholders. Chaplin became Chairman of the London & South Western Railway. With Horne he started a business as carriers for the London & Birmingham Railway. Some provincial proprietors followed suit, such as Matthew in Leeds and Waddell in Birmingham.

Innkeepers were often less fortunate. Some surviveed fairly well, for in many towns the main coaching inns had catered for things other than coaching, such as weddings, banquets and election meetings. Some inns became private houses, such as the Bull's Head (later Royal Sussex Hotel) on the Holyhead road. Inns in villages and small towns suffered most, particularly those bypassed by the railway. Some were converted into shops or banks, the stables into cottages. Otherwise they faded away gradually, and the towns faded with them.

The advantages of railways also became obvious to businessmen. Those in Birmingham in the mid 19th century prided themselves on looking to the future. By the end of 1838 the London & Birmingham and Grand Junction Railways, planned only five years earlier, had connected the place with London, Liverpool and Manchester. Trade and industry were to expand immeasurably. Prior to the railway road carriers had commonly charged around 10d per mile per ton of goods. The much cheaper railway rates show why they quickly superseded the carrier's wagon for long journeys.

The social benefits of the railway were also being realised. By the early 1840s the public saw railways as quicker, cheaper and more comfortable than the road coaches. Rail fares from Birmingham to London varied from 20 to 32 shillings depending on class, while inside fares for a stagecoach were 20 shillings to 30 shillings upwards.

People's expectations of travel were also transformed by railways. Those who believed that man could never travel faster than the speed of a horse could now career across the country at undreamed of speeds of 25 or 30 miles an hour. The public imagination had been captured. During 1837 stage coaches had taken around 50,000 passengers in the whole year from London to Brighton. Railways were to take as many as 73,000 in a single week. There could be no competing with such figures.

Long distance coaches were the first to be taken off, followed by most provincial coaches. In Birmingham and much of the Midlands the stage coach was quickly becoming a thing of the past. This advert appeared in Aris's *Birmingham Gazette* for Monday 16th April 1838.

STAGE COACHES
FOR SALE, 24 new and second-hand very good 4 and
pair-horse coaches, and one light van on springs, at
Wilkes's Coach Manufactory Woodstock, Oxfordshire.

Even so, the effect of the railways on road coaches was not completely straightforward, particularly in large provincial towns like Birmingham. Up to 1835 there were six coaches daily each way between Birmingham and Worcester. When the London & Birmingham Railway opened traffic trebled, because to go from Worcester to London it was best to travel from Worcester to Birmingham by road, then catch a London train.

By 1839 stagecoach traffic between Worcester and Birmingham had increased to 29 per day, but when the Birmingham & Gloucester line was opened in 1841 with a station at Spetchley near Worcester, the coaches ceased overnight.

By 1841 all the Warwick - London runs had vanished, and of the remaining twenty four services, twelve went to Coventry, and seven to Birmingham. The Cambridge service was stopped, and until recently the two towns did not resume direct public transport connections. All public coach services had gone from Warwick by 1850.

Birmingham too had lost all its London routes by the early 1840s. By 1845 there were no London coaches leaving the Hen & Chickens, though the *Tantivy* and *Wonder* were still operating. Coaches ran to only ten destinations, where ten years earlier they had gone to nearly two hundred. At this time the Swan Inn sent coaches to thirteen ultimate destinations, including, Kidderminster and Lichfield. And there were a few surviving mails to Aberystwyth, Holyhead (via Bangor), Shrewsbury and Ludlow.

By 1850 only a handful of coaches left Birmingham, while in Shrewsbury only four or five still ran. Ludlow still had three coaches, including a Royal Mail to Birmingham and a coach to Shrewsbury called the *Engineer*. By 1856 there were no long distance stage coaches running from the main towns of Shropshire. A Shrewsbury newspaper of October 1861 noted:

"The last of the coaches.

The Railways are gradually pushing coaches off the road. The opening of the Worcester and Hereford Railways, besides superseding numberless carrier's carts, has caused 3 mail coaches to be discontinued, via the Worcester and Hereford Royal Mail...Before the Worcester and Hereford line was opened from Worcester to Malvern, about 20 coaches ran daily between Malvern and Worcester, every one of which is now put down."

A couple of short distance stage coaches still ran. The *Railway Queen* was a four horse coach between Builth Wells and Knighton where it connected with trains for Shrewsbury. But there was little else, and coaching was by now a marginal activity.

With the death of the coaches came the death of a whole industry with severe and far reaching effects. Edward Corbett summed up the situation well:

> "It is always a melancholy thing to see any class of men suddenly deprived of their means of subsistence, from no fault of their own. It is very easy to say that if one's trade fails another must be found, and to some political economists this appears to be a sufficient solution...; but it by no means has that effect upon the sufferers. A man who has thoroughly learned one handicraft can very seldom become as proficient in any other."

If a change of employment from one transport system to the other was considered, coach guards were the only men with experience relevant to railway work. Coachmen were usually much less fortunate; the railways had little use for their talents and there is no record of any coachmen finding work on them. A few were lucky enough to find their skills app - reciated in domestic service, others went to drive the ever increasing numbers of omnibuses. Some became innkeepers, but with the rapid decrease in long distance road traffic the innkeeping business was in recession too.

"Smart Tom" Pinner, a coachman from the Birmingham to Cambridge run, took over the Five Ways Tavern in Birmingham. Here "he was well known and respected by nearly everyone ..." George Wild who once drove the *Peveril of the Peak*, finally kept a public house in a village on the Birmingham road. Another Birmingham coachman, Ben Holmes, became a well respected retailer of boots and shoes with the "same merry twinkle about the eye" which had made him so popular driving coaches forty or fifty years earlier.

Some coachmen clung to coaching for as long as possible. Areas where railway development was later than the rest of the country, such as parts of the West Country and Highland Scotland, attracted some of the top coachmen who were able to prolong their careers for a few years.

Bill Tolley stayed with coaching to the very end. After leaving the *Erin-go-Bragh,* he drove the Worcester Mail, the Holyhead and then the Ludlow coaches before becoming a successful omnibus and car proprietor in Hockley, Birmingham. Sam Haywood of the Shrewsbury *Wonder* married a widow, landlady of the Raven & Bell in Shrewsbury, and died in 1851. Barton, a coachman who drove on both the Birmingham and the Dover roads, became a veterinary surgeon. William Clements, one time driver of the *Tally-Ho!* and *Eagle* died in 1891 aged 91.

A few coachmen never recovered from the demise of their industry. Dick Vickers who once drove the Holyhead Mail, tried farming but ended bankrupt. He was eventually driven to despair and killed himself. Perhaps coachmen may have permitted themselves a wry smile at the following quotation by the "Last Stagecoachman" published in *Taits Magazine* - "Mark my words, if there's a last coachman, the time will come when there's a last stoker."

Toll gate receipts had also been falling. After the peak year of 1837 they began to decline. Between London and Birmingham the income of the Holyhead Road Turnpike Trust was reduced by half due to competition from the railway. After a maximum successful bid for the Alcester toll gate of £1,490, the value of the gate fell steadily, so that by 1847 the Alcster Turnpike Trust had to halve its tolls to encourage trade. Within a couple of years of the first Birmingham railways, the Bromsgrove turnpike gate had lost half its revenue, and things got worse.

Only ten years after the start of the main line railways most turnpike trusts were bankrupt. Their debts were such that any takeover and reorganisation by government would have been useless, so they were left to die off naturally. In 1871 there were 854 trusts, by 1890 there were only two. The last toll gates were on the Holyhead road in Anglesey which went out of business in 1895.

Though long distance coaches and carrier's wagons were no longer running, good roads were still necessary for short haul traffic. Care and maintenance reverted to parishes or groups of parishes called Highway Districts, but in 1888 the Local Government Act set up County Councils which became responsible for maintaining all main roads.

By the mid 1850s the coaching era was finished. Coaches were abandoned, broken up and sold as scrap or made into chicken sheds. There is a record of an abandoned coach in the garden of the Noel Arms Inn, at Wishaw in Warwickshire, which survived within the living memory of one of the villagers, but that is a rarity. Some mail coaches were shipped to Spain, where they ran for years from Malaga in the south to Vittoria and Salamanca in the north. But apart from a few coaches scattered around the country in various museums [see Appendix], there is hardly a trace of these vehicles which once dominated the roads. The only public stagecoach in the Midlands is in Birmingham's Museum and Art Gallery. As we mentioned in the Introduction, it was built late in the era, was not typical and came from Liverpool.

Other uses for coaches gradually emerged after they ceased to be commercially viable. Old stagecoaches were brought into use for pleasure excursions and sporting and family outings, and obsolete services were occasionally revived.

One of the main instigators of this coaching revival was the Duke of Beaufort, who began putting on coaches in the early 1860s. In August 1874 Mr W D Claridge ran the *Emperor Alexander Coach and Four* from the Craven Arms, Coventry to the Castle and Falcon, Aldersgate Street, London. In April 1878 Lord Aylesford put on a pleasure coach between Birmingham and Coventry during the Summer months, and in 1880, the *Shakespeare* trotted out on summer mornings from the Regent Hotel, Leamington Spa to Stratford upon Avon.

By the end of the century a few coach services still ran as tourist attractions. The Birmingham & Midland Motor Omnibus Company Ltd (Midland Red) were still running a four in hand to Lilleshaw Hall from the Grand Hotel, Colmore Row, Birmingham as late as 1928. But this was not coaching as it had been in the 1820s and 1830s; nothing approaching those exhilarating days on the road would ever be recaptured.

Since the end of the coaching era the whole pace of life has changed unimaginably. In the *Introduction* I mentioned how people riding the stage were in touch with their natural surroundings, but the distance between us and the environment has now widened to a broad and deep chasm. Our modern experience of travel does not remotely resemble the mystery and magic of the stagecoach.

Glossary of Coaching Terms

Artist: expert coachman

Benjamin: greatcoat worn by coachmen

Bit of Fish: passengers not entered on waybill, or time-sheet

Boot: locker under or forming part of driving seat on horse drawn vehicle; any kind of luggage compartment

Both sides of the road, or **Two Sweats**: team worked up and back down a stage on same day

Box: raised driving seat at front; might be double or single and sometimes held tool kit or valuables

Butterflies: short distance public coaches

Bye Coach: cross country coach

Bye Mail: cross country mail coach

Bye Mails: mail bags sent across country, not via London

Cock Horse: extra horse added to help team up steep hill, usually ridden by postillion

Cross Team: two greys and two darker horses

Dickey Seat: guard's seat at the back of the coach

Drag or Park Coach: private four in hand coach, similar to a stage or mail coach

Drag Shoe or Skid Pan: hollow metal plate fixed to near-side rear wheel when going down steep hills. Later coaches also had a "pressure brake" worked by hand lever or foot pedal

Feather Edging: driving very close

Flash of Lightning: glass of brandy or gin

Footboard: angled board to support driver's feet

Four in Hand: coach hauled by four horses

Hammercloth: protective cover on box seat of some coaches and carriages, often elaborately embroidered

Handling the Ribbons: holding the reins

Jobmaster: hirer out of horses, harness and vehicles; operated from coach office or inn

Kicking Them: asking for a tip

(121)

Leaders: front pair of horses in team
Lower Ground: near destination

Middle Ground: between starting point and destination

Post Boys: small, light men usually attached to posting inn; acted as postillions and when four horses were used for posting, two post boys rode nearside horses
Postillions: grooms or post boys riding one horse on coach. If extra leaders were added to team of four, postillion usually rode nearside leader
Putten 'em to: harnessing the team
Pykie: turnpike gate keeper

Rumble: rearward seat on coach or carriage; found on early stagecoaches as basketwork compartment at back for passengers travelling at cheap rates

Scaly one: passenger giving small tip
Shouldering: not declaring passengers
Splashing Board: shield in front of driver's seat
Springing the Team: making team canter to help climb steep hill
Stones: roads in built up areas
Swallowing pocketing short fares by guards

Tommy: coachman's whip
Tooling: driving pair or team of horses
Turn: section of good turnpike road

Up Mail: mail travelling to London
Upper Ground: near London, or other point of departure

Wheelers: pair of horses nearest coach in team of four or more

Places to Visit

AVONCROFT MUSEUM OF HISTORIC BUILDINGS
Stoke Heath, Bromsgrove, Worcestershire B60 4JR Tel
01527 831886/831363 Fax 01527 876934. Open early
March to late November; there is a toll house.

BIRMINGHAM CITY MUSEUM AND ART GALLERY
Chamberlain Square, Birmingham B3 3DH Tel 0121 235
2834 Fax 0121 236 6227. The Social History section
has a stagecoach built in 1860.

BLIST'S HILL OPEN AIR MUSEUM
Ironbridge, Shropshire. Tel 01952 433522/01952 583003.
Open all year round; has a toll house and bit of turnpike
road.

SCIENCE MUSEUM
Exhibition Road, South Kensington, London. SW7 2DD
0171 938 9732 Fax 0171 938 8118. There is a mail coach
built in 1827 which operated on the London to York
route; see the photo under *The Royal Mail Coach*. In 1877
it ran between Stratford upon Avon and Leamington
Spa as a pleasure coach.

STAFFORDSHIRE COUNTY MUSEUM
Shugborough House, Milford, near Stafford ST17 OXB
Tel 01889 881 388 exts 208/209/211/214 Fax 0889
881323. There is a park drag (private version of
stage coach), private omnibus, hansom cab and more.

Further Reading

[Books are grouped under main themes.]

COACHING & COACHES

The Coaching Age, Mountfield D (Robert Hale & Co 1976)
Coaching Days of England, Burgess A (Paul Elek 1966)
The Coaching Life, Hanson H (Manchester University
    Press 1983)
Coventry Coaching and Coach Roads, Whitley T W (Coventry
    Library 1888)
Downhill Journey: Stage Coaching in Shrewsbury 1833-1861,
    Evason C in Victorian Shrewsbury Research Group's
    Victorian Shrewsbury (Shropshire Libraries 1984)
Coaching City: A Glimpse of Georgian Lichfield, Clayton
    H (E J Morton 1970)
Discovering Horse Drawn Vehicles, Smith D J (Shire 1994)

GENERAL HISTORIES

Old and New Birmingham, Dent R *(Houghton and Hammond
    1880, Reprinted 1972 by E P Publishing)*
A History of Warwickshire, Slater T (Phillimore & Co
    Ltd 1981)

HIGHWAYMEN

Stage Coach and Highwayman, Holroyd S V (Coventry
    Library 1963)
Hero on a Stolen Horse, Evans H & M (Frederic Muller
    Ltd 1977)

ROYAL MAIL

*A More Expeditious Conveyance: The Story of the Royal
    Mail Coaches*, Rider B (J A Allen 1984)

ROADS

The Archaeology of the Transport Revolution 1750-1850,
    Ransom P J G (World's Work Ltd 1984)
Roads and Vehicles, Bird A (Arrow 1973)
The Old Roads of England, Addison Sir William (Batsford
    1980)
The Turnpike Road System in England, Albert W (Cambridge
    University Press 1972)
Roads of Worcestershire Vol II, Gwilliam H W (Worcester
    Library 1987)